Man and Boy

A play

Terence Rattigan

Foreword by David Suchet
Director's Note by Maria Aitken

Samuel French — London
New York - Toronto - Hollywood

MAN AND BOY

The Yvonne Arnaud Theatre, Guildford, production, presented by Thelma Holt, Bill Kenwright and Nica Burns for Theatreshare plc and Michael Whitehall, at the Duchess Theatre, London, 2005 with following cast:

Carol Penn	Jennifer Lee Jellicorse
Basil Anthony	Ben Silverstone
Sven Johnson	David Yelland
Gregor Antonescu	David Suchet
Mark Herries	Colin Stinton
David Beeston	Will Huggins
Countess Antonescu (Florence)	Helen Grace

Directed by Maria Aitken
Designed by Simon Higlett
Lighting by Mick Hughes
Sound and music by Howard Davidson

COPYRIGHT INFORMATION

(See also page ii)

CHARACTERS

Carol Penn
Basil Anthony
Gregor Antonescu
Sven Johnson
Mark Herries
David Beeston
Countess Antonescu

The action of the play takes place in a basement apartment
in Greenwich Village, New York

Time: continuous, roughly between 6pm and 8.30pm on
a July night in 1934

FOREWORD BY DAVID SUCHET

I was first offered the role of Gregor Antonescu in *Man and Boy* in 1993. Since then it came my way three more times and on each occasion I declined the offer. However, in January 2004, I was offered the role yet again. And said "yes".

There are many reasons for turning down a role and surprisingly very few reasons for saying "yes". Up until my final offer I just did not feel sufficient passion for the role, nor did I feel ready to play the kind of irredeemable villain that epitomizes Gregor Antonescu. In January 2004 I was ready on both counts.

Geoffrey Wansell's account of the history of *Man and Boy* in his most interesting biography of Terence Rattigan affected me deeply. Also, the very fact that *Man and Boy* was Rattigan's attempt at a come-back which he considered most important and which completely failed. The wounds he felt as a result of the play's rejection were never healed. The above, coupled with my feelings that the play had more relevance in 2004 than I felt it had in 1964 when it was first performed, also contributed to my feeling passionate about wanting to revive the play. It was in danger of becoming one of Rattigan's lost works. My *raison d'être* as an actor is first and foremost to serve my writers and I felt I wanted to give Terence Rattigan a better deal.

Our production started a British tour in the Autumn of 2004 and subsequently went into the Duchess Theatre for its West End run. This time the play received a rapturous reception. As a result of this, the play is now back in print and will also become part of Terence Rattigan's performance repertoire.

My sincere hope is that one day I will have the great pleasure of sitting amongst the audience enjoying another production of this extraordinary play by Terence Rattigan.

David Suchet

DIRECTOR'S NOTE

I first read *Man and Boy* in 2003, trawling through the drama section of the London Library. Of course, by the new millennium, Rattigan's reputation had been reinstated with more revivals than at any time since the nineteen fifties; his plays are back in print; there are three biographies — so I was curious at the neglect of this particular play. Rattigan had considered it his masterpiece, but it had a disappointing critical reception in both London and New York and so far had never been seen again.

I took it to the producer Michael Whitehall, and we agreed that, while flawed, it haunted us, and the fulcrum of the play, intended to be shocking, still kept its potency — a rare thing in period plays. Soon after, David Suchet approached us, saying he had been offered the part three times before (in productions that never happened) but had always turned it down. Now, however, he felt the play — and the part — were too good to remain neglected. I had no doubt that he had the courage to embody Antonescu's dark side unflinchingly, as his predecessor in the role, Charles Boyer, apparently had not. In fact Rattigan said bitterly that he had played the part "like a head waiter". David and I agreed that our mission would be to get *Man and Boy* back into the repertoire.

One of Rattigan's biographers, Michael Darlow, alerted us to the existence of ten previous drafts of the play. There followed a fascinating period in the British Library, much aided by Curator of Modern Manuscripts, Sally Brown. It seemed to me that some of Rattigan's earliest ideas had been his finest and many of the later changes were probably brought about by commercial pressures. With permission from the Rattigan estate, I compiled a version principally drawn from four early drafts and the final one that played in New York.

I fully expected the shade of Rattigan to rise up and smite me as I directed his rearranged play — but he did not. In fact his own words to Binkie Beaumont seem a plea to posterity to give *Man and Boy* another life: " ... will this new play be good or bad? Nothing else matters. Nothing at all. Because, if you ... don't like the play ... it will still probably be published ... and possibly, be read by some historian of the theatre in fifty years time and pronounced as 'the best work of a fashionable contemporary dramatist: ironically it wasn't performed in his lifetime.' That would be sufficient reward for my labours, even though I, perforce, had to read the review in heaven."

I hope he did look down and read his reviews: they were marvellous. And above all, I hope *Man and Boy* will now take its rightful place in the Rattigan canon and receive many more revivals.

Maria Aitken. London, February 2006.

ACT I

1934. A summer's evening about six p.m.

Basil Anthony's basement apartment in Greenwich Village, New York, a rather sleazy neighbourhood

There are two rooms. One room is a barely furnished living-room with a kitchenette.The front door opens directly from the living-room and steps lead up to street level. The other is the adjoining bedroom which has a door leading to a shower and a lavatory

A girl, Carol Penn, lies in a bed under a sheet and coverlet. She is smoking a cigarette. In the shower, a boy, Basil Anthony, in a state of semi-dress is gargling. His hair is still dripping from the shower. He finishes gargling , rubs a towel over his hair and then begins to comb it. Carol puts out her cigarette and looks at a watch on the bedside table

Carol is American. Basil speaks with an English accent

Carol Hey, do you know it's nearly six? Are you going to be in there all day?

No reply

> I've never known anyone take longer showers than you. There's some-thing symbolical in washing yourself as clean as that. Like the play I'm in you haven't even bothered to see. That's symbolical. So symbolical it's off on Saturday. Where's my bathrobe?

Basil (*moving in to the bedroom*) *Your* bathrobe?
Carol My usual.
Basil I hung it up.

Basil takes the bathrobe off a hook on the wall and throws it to Carol. He gets dressed during the following

> I thought the Federal Theatre Project had promised you a minimum three weeks.

Carol (*going in to the shower*) They didn't promise us anything. They just said how lucky we were not to be starving like all the other actors in New

York, and how we all ought to get on our knees every night to President
Roosevelt and the Federal Theatre Project etcetera, etcetera. For a week's
run on Second Avenue I should get on my knees?

Basil You should.

Carol What?

Basil (*shouting back*) You should get on your knees to Equity and President
Roosevelt and the Federal Theatre Project and the W.P.A. etcetera,
etcetera.

Carol But you hate President Roosevelt.

Basil I don't hate him. I just don't happen to think he's going far enough fast
enough, that's all.

Carol You goddamn Bolshie.

Basil Ok, so I'm a goddamn Bolshie. I'm going to the corner to get a paper.

Carol Why?

Basil Because I want to see the news, that's why.

Carol (*still in shower area*) What's gotten into you this afternoon? You're
acting like you got fired or something. You haven't, have you?

Basil Haven't what?

Carol That's just what I mean. All afternoon you've been acting like I wasn't
here.

Basil Well, I don't know about you but I've had rather a good afternoon.

Carol No. No complaints about that. (*Pause*) You haven't got fired, have
you?

Basil (*going towards the living-room*) No. As a matter of fact, I got a raise.

Carol No kidding!

Basil I'm up to twenty-six dollars a week now.

Carol Bloated capitalist. And just for playing the piano in a crummy joint.

Basil It's not a crummy joint. You thought it very high class, remember? And
now I'm playing three times a night — they've added a dinner session.

Carol Why didn't you tell me?

Basil I didn't think of it.

Carol That's what I mean. This afternoon you're not with me.

Basil (*at the front-door*) I'm not with you now.

Basil exits

*Carol, from the shower, begins to sing. The telephone rings. Carol, bath-
towel wrapped round her, comes to answer it*

Carol Hallo, Gramercy 73961. ... No, but he'll be back in a moment. Shall
I get him to call you? Or would you like to leave ——

The telephone is abruptly disconnected

— a message, you heel.

Carol returns to the shower and sings. Unseen, she is dressing as far as a slip petticoat

Basil enters through the front-door reading a newspaper

(*Calling from the shower*) Did I hear you come in?
Basil Yes.
Carol You must have run.

Basil, not answering, finishes what he is reading and then impatiently stuffs the whole paper into the waste-paper basket. He pours himself a stiff bourbon and water from the drinks trolley

(*Continuing blithely*) Can I tell you something? It's not just this afternoon you're not with me. In six months you never have been with me — all that much. (*She comes out of the shower wearing the bathrobe over her slip*)
Basil I don't know what you mean by that.
Carol Today you don't tell me you've got a raise. So when have you ever told me anything about yourself, except that you're English and play the piano and haven't got any folks ——
Basil I'm not English.
Carol What are you then?
Basil American.
Carol Sure. All of two months American. What were you then? Listen, I can tell an English accent, honey. I see Ronald Coleman pictures ...

Carol moves into the living-room at the exact moment that Basil, having finished his drink, is getting another

Yeah. That's my Basil.
Basil It's my whisky if I want to drink it.
Carol Sure. It's your life too if you want to shorten it.
Basil You exaggerate abominably.
Carol Exaggerate abominably! Gee, I go for the way you talk. (*She points to his drink*) How many does that make?
Basil We're not married yet.
Carol *Yet*? (*She kisses him*)

Basil returns the kiss

Does that mean you haven't finally turned me down?
Basil We haven't enough money to get married.
Carol Come the end of the Depression, I'll be keeping you. (*She spots the newspaper in the basket*) Unless you keep up this millionaire stuff of throwing papers away. It's today's, isn't it? I haven't even seen it, I would have gone and bought another ——

Basil There wasn't anything in it. (*He finishes his drink and puts the glass down*)

Carol is staring at the headline

Carol Wasn't anything in it? This is serious, isn't it? If this guy Antonescu crashes, I mean?
Basil Yes.
Carol (*going to the bedroom*) He's the greatest, isn't he?
Basil Yes.
Carol Didn't he save the pound or something?
Basil No.
Carol Some currency he saved.
Basil The franc in 1926.
Carol (*shrugging off her bathrobe and stepping into a dress*) So he's the one who rescued Europe after the war?
Basil Yes.
Carol If he goes down, we'll all be out of work. I suppose you're delighted.
Basil D-delighted?
Carol (*sitting on the bed and putting on shoes*) You want the capitalist system to crash, don't you? Put the radio on, honey.

Basil puts on the radio . We hear the strains of Guy Lombardo. Basil picks up his abandoned drink

Basil Not necessarily *want* it to crash. I just know it's going to, that's all, and probably very soon. Certainly before the thirties are out. And when it does, there'll be a better system to take it's place.
Carol (*applying lipstick*) So you're delighted if Antonescu goes the way of the rest — Insull, Stavisky ...
Basil I'm not d-delighted ——
Carol Why not? He's a capitalist, isn't he? Zip me up, will you?
Basil (*going in to the bedroom*) B-but a rather d-different kind of capitalist. He a sort of v-visionary — a Keynesian economist really ...
Carol What's with the stammer all of a sudden? (*She takes the glass from his hand*) Looks like you've had enough of that, honey.

Basil allows her to take it

Why do you do it?

No reply

Why do you dislike yourself so much?

She draws him down to sit beside her on the bed, puts her arms around him. No reply

You're the only person in the world who does, you know. And me, frankly,
I love you.

No reply

I know you need me. What are you so scared of?

*On the radio we hear "Six p.m. BULOVA. Bulova Watch Time. Every hour
on the hour, the New York Times brings you important news bulletins."*

Basil makes a move towards the living-room to turn the radio off

Carol No. Let's hear it.

*On the radio: "All day sensational rumours regarding the impending
collapse of the financial empire of Gregor Antonescu, Roumanian-born
radio and oil king, have been coming in minute by minute. It has been hard
to separate fact from fiction, but this much is known."*

Come back here. It was kind of nice the way we were.

Basil comes back and sits beside her on the bed

> *During the following, Sven Johnson silently enters through the unlocked
> front-door, which he closes carefully behind him. He is an elegantly
> dressed man of middle-age, carrying a briefcase. He listens impassively to
> the voice of the radio announcer*

*On the radio: "The crisis began late last night when first reports hit Wall
Street that a merger planned between one of Antonescu's concerns, Manson
Radios, with the great combine American Electric, has failed. Today a wave
of selling has flooded the market and stockmarkets all over the world have
reported panic unloading of all Antonescu shares. The crash, if it should
come, will be much the biggest in financial history."*

What'd I tell you? Poor guy. The poor guy.
Basil (*suddenly fierce*) Don't be so sure.

*On the radio: "The international banker, Mr J.P. Morgan, said an hour ago
that Antonescu had undoubtedly overextended himself with loans to many
European countries and the failure of Antonescu's merger with American
Electric was merely the last straw – a straw that not only has shown which
way the wind is blowing, but has also, perhaps, broken the camel's back."*

Carol He's mixing his metaphors a bit, isn't he?

On the radio: "Of the financier himself, Gregor Antonescu, so called Saviour and mystery man of Europe — nothing has been heard since he was photographed leaving his Long Island mansion for the Antonescu Building on Wall Street early this morning. But there have been several rumours as to his whereabouts — none of them confirmed as yet."

Sven has grown impatient and abruptly turns off the radio. In the bedroom, Basil and Carol look at each other, puzzled. Sven turns to the bedroom

Sven (*calling gently*) Vassily?

Basil jumps to his feet and stands stiffly, making no move towards the door

Carol Who's that?
Sven (*calling, with more authority*) Vassily?

Basil now moves towards the door very slowly. It is plain to us and to Carol that he knows the owner of the voice

Carol Who is it?

Basil doesn't reply. He may not even have heard her. He goes into the living-room, staring at his visitor. During the following, Carol moves to the living-room doorway

Sven Good-evening, Vassily.
Basil (*at length*) Get out. You're not wanted here. Get out.
Sven Could we talk in private?
Basil No, because we're not going to talk at all.
Sven You mustn't try and use violence, dear boy.
Basil You got the thugs outside?
Sven Your manners haven't improved. Sergei and William have been promoted since your time. William is even President of a bank ——
Basil But they still carry guns?
Sven These are violent times. You must know how many attempts have been made on the life of — (*he looks at Carol*) our mutual friend. Anyway, they're not outside. Tonight I'm the bodyguard.
Basil You're not going to use force on me ...
Sven No, of course not. If it gives you pleasure to hit me, I shall simply stand here and let you. (*With a faint smile*) Perhaps *lie* here, after you've done your worst. (*He eyes Basil's slight figure and smiles again*) But I'm not leaving this apartment until I've said what I have to say.

Basil stands hesitant

(*After a few moments, he nods at Carol*) Would you introduce me?

Carol I'm Carol Penn.

Sven I'm Sven Johnson. How do you do. I have some matters of great urgency to talk over with Vassily here ——

Carol Basil?

Sven Basil? Yes. Stupid of me. With Mr Anthony here.

Basil At least you've got the surname right.

Sven Yes. I should have had the Christian name too.

Basil And you knew the address?

Sven Oh yes. That's been known for a long time. Also the phone number. I called earlier and having established you were here, I thought I'd better come and explain things myself. (*To Carol*) Miss Penn, I wonder if I could trouble you ——

Basil She's not going. You can say what you want to in front of her.

Sven Won't that embarrass you — Basil?

Basil Do you think she hasn't guessed already?

Carol Well, frankly, I hadn't — but well — maybe I'm beginning to get thoughts I shouldn't — maybe, in fact, I'd better get — the hell ——

Basil No. Stay here. Don't leave me alone. (*To Sven*) All right. Tell me. What does father want?

Sven Just a shelter for the night.

Basil God —he must have his hideouts ——

Sven No. Only known places of residence and there are reporters watching all of them. This — situation — wasn't envisaged, you see ——

Basil Christ — it should have been. I envisaged it five years ago — when I was eighteen. And if you — and the great master-minds round him — didn't see this thing coming ——

Sven Your father inspires great faith, you know.

Basil Sure I know. In everyone else, but not in me.

Sven You were always such a pessimist, Vassily.

Basil A paper empire. It stood out a mile, even then.

Sven Currency is paper, you know. And any piece of paper signed by your father has always been far more valuable than currency. We haven't dropped dividends — even in '30 and '31.

Basil Dividends paid out of capital ——

Sven A bit of shifting of assets from time to time. But all quite sound — essentially sound.

Basil (*scornfully*) *Sound*? It looks like it now, doesn't it?

Sven (*with conviction*) We'll come through, you know.

Basil You don't believe that, do you?

Sven Yes. I believe it.

Basil (*bitterly*) Because father says so?

Sven I know of no better reason. Do you?

Basil Yes. Facts. (*He points to the radio*) What I heard tonight.

Sven We went through something almost as bad over the Hoover moratorium. It only took him a week to straighten that out.

Basil Then why doesn't he face the press and tell them that in a week's time he'll be back again — on top of the world?

Sven I've no doubt he will, in due course. Tonight he's very tired. He hasn't slept in three nights, you know.

Basil I wonder he's slept any night at all in the last ten years.

Sven He's tired to death, Vassily. I've been with him every minute since the crisis broke, and I know. It's I who stopped him facing the press today. It's a terrible strain on a man to have to smile and smile ——

Basil And be a villain.

Sven That came out very aptly. It quite reminded me of the old days. But your father isn't a villain, Vassily — and you know it.

Basil Then why is he behaving like one now? Why is he hiding out like some common little gangster on the run? Why is he in such straits that he even wants to come here?

Sven I don't think you've ever understood what he feels about you, Vassily ——

Basil No. I haven't — ever — understood ——

Sven Your leaving him was the greatest shock of his life ——

Basil Not the greatest. Not even a very big shock. But it must have been a shock all right. The emperor had to acknowledge a defeat. A small one — but a defeat ——

Sven You've grown very cynical in your five years.

Basil Grown up, perhaps.

Sven I don't think it's grown-up to deny that there might be other reasons for a father to feel unhappy at being deserted by his only son. However, don't let's argue. At this moment he wants shelter. And are you going to refuse it?

Carol Where is Basil's — Vassily's — father now?

Sven In that square, two blocks away. I don't know what it's called ——

Carol Washington Square. Isn't that dangerous?

Sven No. It's getting dark. He's sitting on a bench. No-one would believe ——

Carol You're goddamn right no-one would believe. A park bench! (*To Basil*) Your idea he should stay there all night?

Basil (*wildly*) There *must* be places — there are small hotels — Turkish baths ——

Carol He'd be recognized for sure. That face has been on the front page of every paper these last three days. Plenty of times before that, too.

Sven Besides, it's vital for him to use the telephone tonight, and there is no other place that is safe. (*To Basil*) That is all quite apart from the paternal reasons I told you ——

Basil (*interrupting harshly*) Leave out the paternal reasons. All right. He can have this apartment for tonight. But I won't be here.

Sven He'll be very sad to hear it.

Basil Tell him I have to go and work.

Sven Ah yes. At the *Green Hat.*

Basil (*furiously*) Sure, at the *Green Hat.* I suppose he knows what I get paid there, too? Who my friends are? What music I play?

Sven (*faintly amused*) I should think it's all in the dossier ——

Basil Dossier! Oh, my God! The Antonescu Intelligence system. I might have guessed. Here. (*He throws Sven a key*) Give that to the saviour of post-war Europe with my blessing. Tell him I won't disturb him — sorry, *upset* him by coming in later. I'll sleep out.

Sven shrugs and nods. He turns to leave through the front-door and moves up the steps

(*Shouting after him*) And keep him out of here for ten minutes. That's all I ask. Just ten minutes and I'll be clear.

Sven I'll tell him. He'll be sad.

Sven exits

Basil moves swiftly to the bedroom, puts on a bow tie and dinner jacket

Carol (*following him, from the doorway*) I don't think you should run out.

Basil (*savagely*) Oh, don't you? God — you don't know ——

Carol No, obviously I don't. But I don't think you should run out now. (*Coming in*)You won't feel too good about it tomorrow.

Basil (*bitterly*) You mean, "I'll hate myself in the morning"?

Carol Sure. Things can be true you know, even if they do say them in the movies ... (*Shrugging*) You're European and maybe I'm just a sentimental American. But the guy seems to be in trouble, he seems to be your father, and he seems to need help.

Basil Oh, for Christ's sake, shut up.

Carol You could have told me. I can be trusted. I wish you had told me.

Basil I couldn't tell anyone. Not anyone. Not even you. Get it?

Carol Yes.

Basil I'd better go. Coming?

Carol (*tidying the bed*) Hold on a second. Look at the bed, we don't want him to get the wrong idea.

Basil laughs

What's so funny?

Basil Wrong idea. He thinks I'm queer anyway.

Carol (*finishing the bed*) No kidding. Were you ever? I mean — schoolboy stuff?

Basil No.

Carol Then why ——

Basil You've said it sometimes. I'm too soft. Come on.

Carol (*peering at him*) Do you have any eye-wash?

Basil Yes.

He goes to the bathroom and we see him apply eyewash and towel

Carol (*keeping it matter-of-fact*) Your mother alive?

Basil No. She died when I was two.

Carol Tough. Wasn't she a famous actress? Didn't I read somewhere ——

Basil She was a French chorus girl. A stripper, if you must know. Yes. They had them — in Bucharest music halls — even in those days — only they didn't call it stripping, they just came on and stripped and stayed stripped.

Pause

Carol Your father tell you that?

Basil Who else?

Pause

Carol He married again, didn't he?

Basil He wasn't *married* to my mother.

Carol Ah. Well, I know there's a present Mrs Antonescu.

Basil Countess Antonescu.

Carol Ever met her?

Basil Since my time. I gather she was a typist from the London pool.

Carol Why the title?

Basil He bought it. Holy Roman Empire.

Carol Doesn't that make him a Count?

Basil He won't use it for himself. He says the name Gregor Antonescu needs no appendage, and shall I tell you something? He's right. (*Coming back into the bedroom*) Better now?

Carol Yes. You can duck out with dignity now.

Basil Duck out?

Carol That's what I said.

Basil (*quietly*) My God! Of course, I should have seen it. Ducking out is exactly what he'll expect from me. The little boy who was scared of horses, and wouldn't learn to swim and ran away from everything. Always ran away. (*Beat*) OK, you win.

Carol Do what you think is right.

Basil picks up the telephone and dials

Carol goes out of the front-door and up the steps. She pauses for a moment and then comes swiftly back in, closing the door. Meanwhile, Basil has suffered a crisis of confidence and replaced the phone

Carol They're at the end of the block. Honey, if you're going, go.
Basil I'm not going. (*He dials again*)
Carol (*coming to bedroom door*) Do you want me to go?
Basil No. (*bitterly*) I wouldn't deprive you of the thrill of meeting Gregor Antonescu in the flesh.
Carol That's a bit of a low blow, isn't it?
Basil Sorry. (*Into the phone*) Hallo, Sam. Is Joe in the club? ... Get him for me, will you? ... Sure, I'll hold on.

Sven comes down the stairs, only partially seen. A key turns in the lock and he enters. He looks round the room, sees Carol and shrugs indifferently. Then he stands back, a shade obsequiously

Gregor Antonescu comes down the steps. He is wearing a black hat, low over his face, and a light overcoat with the collar turned up. As he removes the hat and lowers the collar we see a face that is smooth and relaxed. If it shows signs of fatigue it is the fatigue of an athlete rather than of a man on the verge of losing a billion-dollar empire. He looks around the room with quick interest. Then he sees Carol and bows politely

Sven This is Miss Carol Penn.
Gregor How do you do.
Carol How do you do.
Gregor My name is Antonescu.
Carol I knew that.
Sven Miss Penn will not be staying long.
Gregor I'm so sorry. Please don't go on our account.
Carol (*floundering*) Well — it's this way, you see, Mr Antonescu — I promised Basil — I mean Vassily — your son ——
Gregor Excuse me. (*He takes off his coat and gives it to Sven. Then he sits down*
Basil (*quietly in to the telephone*) Joe? Basil. I can't make the dinner session. Something important ...
Gregor (*to Sven*) I would like a glass of wine.
Sven (*to Carol*) Is there any wine here?
Carol No, I don't think so ——

Basil (*into the telephone*) No, *really* important ... Vital, even.

Sven It doesn't matter what wine. I don't think your son keeps any wine here.

Basil (*into the telephone*) Can you do it for me and I'll do your session tomorrow? ...

Gregor Perhaps some vermouth?

Basil Thanks, pal. Thanks a lot.

Carol I don't think he has that either.

Gregor What does he keep?

Carol Well, there's bourbon over there — and I know he's got some gin——

Gregor Unimpeachably American. But for the village and Vassily, I should have thought a little bourgeois. (*Nodding to Sven*) A bourbon and water. No ice.

Carol I'll get it.

Sven (*sharply*) No!

Carol Afraid I'll poison it?

Gregor I much enjoy American wisecracks. And it is absurd, isn't it? Sven watches over me like an hysterical mother. (*Beat*) But there *have* been attempts to poison me — how many is it, Sven, over the years?

Sven (*pouring the drink*) Seven.

Gregor Not to mention an attempted machine-gunning once — in Berlin — and a very clever attempt to run me over with a truck. That was in Paris, I think.

Sven Here in New York. April '31.

Gregor A wonderful memory he has. And tonight, of all nights, there must be at least a thousand people, all of them bitter enemies, all of them powerful and all of them capable of murder, to whom my death would come as a pleasurable surprise. From that list I entirely exclude you, Miss Penn. I can only apologize that Sven doesn't. (*He drains the glass*)

Sven Another?

Gregor No. Now, Herries is coming here?

Sven Yes. At seven. He's coming from his club, he had to cancel a dinner engagement.

Gregor Did he seem surprised at the address?

Sven No. I simply gave it to him. I told him it was a basement apartment.

Gregor (*suddenly angry, but without raising his voice*) The President of American Electric summoned at night to a basement apartment in Greenwich Village without any explanation?

Sven I thought he would naturally assume you had every reason for conducting the negotiations in the strictest secrecy ——

Gregor (*looking around in distaste*) A park bench in Washington Square would be better.

Sven I'm very sorry G.A. I should have made some excuse.

Gregor I can't imagine anything making a worse impression. We shall have to think of something before he comes. You stopped him issuing that statement?

Sven Yes, but he would only postpone it. Three hours. It has to catch the morning press.
Gregor Did he give you a copy?
Sven No, but I bought it from one of the typists, it only cost a thousand dollars.

Basil moves just inside the living-room staring at Gregor. Carol goes over to Gregor and touches his arm, trying to attract his attention to his son's presence in the room. Gregor now looks up and sees Basil

Gregor Vassily!
Basil Hallo, father.
Gregor (*apparently struggling with his emotions*) My dearest boy, let me say only this. It is hard to tell you what happiness it gives me to see you once again.
Basil (*moving further away*) You've been in New York since January and made no effort to see me.
Gregor Ah, my dear boy, the pressures of business ——
Basil And you've been in New York at least t-ten t-times in the last five years and you've never even tried to get in touch with me ——
Gregor Nor have you with me, *carissimo mio.*
Basil You know why.
Gregor Yes, I know why.

Pause

Basil (*to Sven*) I've put off my dinner session. At the *Green Hat.*
Gregor (*absently*) Have you, dear boy? Why?
Basil To be with you ——
Gregor How kind. How very, very kind. What happiness you give me with such a gesture ——

Basil abruptly turns to get himself a drink, watched solicitously by Carol who makes no effort to interfere

(*Turning to Sven ; in a perfectly level voice*) I believe I have thought of an excuse for Herries. A good one.
Basil (*making an effort*) Do you want some food, father?
Gregor (*smiling at him*) Dearest boy, no. I have reached a stage of exhaustion where the effort of eating would only exhaust me further ——
Basil Shouldn't you go to bed?
Gregor Yes, later I will. But now I must carry on a little longer.
Basil (*approaching him*) You — look — very tired, father.

Gregor (*touching Basil*) I *am* very tired, *carissimo*. How good of you to care.

Carol Can I ask you a question, Mr Antonescu?

Gregor Of course.

Carol Your son isn't the most informative person in the world, you know ——

Gregor Yes, I know.

Carol *He* disowned *you*?

Gregor Correct.

Carol Five years ago?

Gregor Correct.

Carol Why?

Gregor (*shrugging*) At his coming of age party — in Roumania a son comes of age at eighteen — we had words.

Carol They must have been important words.

Gregor (*looking at Basil*) They were.

Carol What were they about?

Gregor Truth and falsehood. Do you know any words more important than those ?

Carol No — I don't.

Basil (*quietly*) Why don't you tell her I tried to kill you?

Pause

Gregor (*equally quietly*) For a very simple reason, dear boy. You didn't.

Basil I fired ——

Gregor (*interrupting with cold authority*) And missed. Any further questions, Miss Penn? (*Before waiting for an answer, to Sven*) I forgot to ask you. Did you get in touch with my wife?

Sven Yes, I found her at the Plaza Hotel. She has been waiting there for over an hour.

Gregor Why?

Sven You called her from Long Island on Friday and arranged an appointment there.

Gregor Did I? Well. Anyway, she should have realized from today's papers, at least, that I could hardly have kept it. (*Remembering Basil's presence*) I have taken the liberty of asking your — er — well, stepmother, shall we call her? — to come here tonight. It is important for a particular reason. I hope you don't mind.

Basil No, of course not.

Gregor You will get on very well with her. She is adorable. (*To Sven*) How have you arranged for her to arrive here without being followed?

Sven Sergei is looking after it. He believes the reporters don't know about the stairs to the apartment below. If she uses that and takes the subway ——

Gregor It is hard to imagine a more conspicuous sight than Florence on the subway.

Sven Sergei said he would see she was suitably dressed.

Gregor A raincoat with a ruby and diamond belt, I expect. It's a big risk but I need her here tonight.

Carol switches the radio on, music blares

(*Flicking his fingers imperiously*) Please turn that off. I'm so sorry, Miss Penn. Music hath charms but destroys concentration.

Carol (*switching off the radio*) I thought you might like to hear the news ——

Gregor Why should I? I know the news and I hate hearing it distorted.

The telephone rings in the bedroom

Sven This may be London. I have your permission, dear Vassily?

Basil Of course.

Sven goes into the bedroom. He picks up the receiver

Carol Mr Antonescu?

Gregor Yes, Miss Penn?

Carol When you said just now that you didn't like hearing the news distorted by the radio announcer, do you mean that the news isn't as bad as it seems?

Sven (*into the telephone*) Transatlantic? Yes. ... yes. ... I'll hold on.

Gregor Well, Miss Penn, it would be ridiculous for me to claim that panic selling of all my shares on all exchanges in the world makes the real news exactly joyful. But if you have any money to invest I think you would help yourself to a fairly agreeable profit if you buy Antonescu shares early tomorrow morning. Manson radio would be best, although any will do. But be early. Later in the day they won't be easy to buy. (*Offhandedly*) You do that too, Vassily, or does your new social conscience forbid it?

Basil Is my new social conscience in the dossier too?

Gregor My dearest boy, I have always known how strong your conscience is. That it should now incline more to Karl Marx than God the Father could possibly have guessed.

Basil I'm not a Marxist.

Gregor What are you?

Basil A socialist.

Gregor I never quite know the difference, except that with Stalin I can do business and with Ramsey MacDonald I can't. Stalin — now there's a man after my own heart. I find him a very level-headed business man ——

Basil What about the labour camps?

Gregor (*shrugging*) Transition period. (*To Carol*) So buy those shares, Miss
Penn — I implore you.
Carol I haven't any money to invest.
Gregor What a pity.

A beat, during which we hear Sven next door

Sven (*into the telephone*) Thank you. I will continue to hold.
Carol But if I had I don't know if — I mean, excuse me, Mr Antonescu, but
it does seem — as of this moment — like you've got a pretty serious crisis
on your hands.
Gregor Oh, yes. I have. As of this moment. That is a good phrase. American
idiom?

Carol nods

I must remember it. Well, Miss Penn, as of this moment, I have got a serious
crisis, yes. A crisis of confidence and of liquidity — exactly the same crisis
as our world economy is passing through today.
Sven (*into the phone*) Lord Thornton, Johnson here.
Gregor But *passing* through, I'm happy to say, thanks to your great
President. I'm going to pass through mine, and by tomorrow morning I
shall have.
Carol What is liquidity?
Gregor Liquidity?
Sven (*calling through to Gregor*) London is on the line.
Gregor (*ignoring him*) A short definition is ready access to cash. Liquidity
and confidence are really the same problem. You have some money in that
charming handbag?
Carol A dollar, fifty cents ...
Gregor I didn't ask how much. But since you have been kind enough to tell
me we can say that, as far as your fare home tonight is concerned, you are
enviably liquid.
Sven (*raising his voice a little*) Lord Thornton is on the line from London,
G.A.
Gregor Liquidity is the lifeblood of our economy, Miss Penn. Since '29 our
financial arteries have hardened and the blood no longer circulates nearly
as freely as it should. The whole capitalist system is in danger of
arteriosclerosis — sick unto death, some say. Many say. Well, Miss Penn,
I don't. I am an optimist — perhaps the only one — in my position — left
in the whole wide world. I believe the crisis is past.
Carol What about your own crisis?
Gregor Exactly the same as the world's. You must get Vassily to explain to
you what liquidity really means, Vassily has a very good financial brain.

(*He goes into the bedroom, closing the door; to Sven*) Before Herries arrives the girl must go.

Sven (*looking at his watch*) She will be leaving anyway in a few moments. Understudies have to report half an hour before curtain time. I checked.

Carol (*studying Basil*) I'll make you some coffee. You need it. (*She moves into the kitchenette to fill the kettle and light the stove etc.*)

Gregor (*picking up the receiver at length; into the telephone*) My dear Thornton. ... How good to hear your voice. Forgive me, dear fellow, I will be with you in just one minute. Keep the line open please, and have the balance sheet of Manson Radios ready, if you would be so kind. (*He puts the receiver on the bedside table and stretches out full length on the bed, in an utterly relaxed attitude*) We will make it two minutes, I think. Wake me if I sleep.

Sven What about the boy. Shouldn't I get rid of him before Herries arrives?

Gregor (*murmuring*) No.

Sven Won't he be a nuisance?

Gregor (*sleepily*) No.

Carol moves and perches on the sofa next to Basil

Carol (*affectionately*) Well, tough guy ——

Basil (*bitterly*) Tough guy.

Carol To up and leave that father? Does anyone come tougher than that? Wow, what a charmer. I guess he's a kind of genius.

Basil I guess he is.

Carol With you he's different, in a funny way. Of course I can see right through all that dearest boy, *carissimo* stuff ——

Basil And what do you see? Contempt?

Carol I wouldn't say that. That's what you like to think he feels because you feel it yourself about yourself. He sees through you OK — that's for sure.

Basil You mean he looks through me — as if I weren't there ——

Carol Oh, no. For him you're there all right. I meant he sees through you.

Basil What does he see?

Carol How you worship him

Pause. Basil stares at her, frowning

Basil I haven't seen my father for five years. I could have called him at any time and been welcomed back with open arms. But I haven't, have I? I've lived in Greenwich Village as a piano player, and on Sundays I've sometimes waved a red flag and shouted slogans which can only mean: "Down with Gregor Antonescu". Now, how, to a rational judge, can that add up to worship?

Carol Perhaps the rational judge hasn't seen the way you look at him when he's in the same room.

Carol goes back into the kitchenette. Basil moodily studies some piano music. In the bedroom, Sven has gently touched Gregor. If Gregor was asleep he is perfectly controlled and alert as he nods to Sven and picks up the receiver from the floor

Gregor (*into the phone*) My dear Thornton, so sorry to have kept you waiting. You, and my other London associates would have had, I imagine, an anxious day. ... I? My dear fellow, I am so much more accustomed to these little disturbances, '31 was just as bad, you know, and '29 was even worse. ... Yes, that is correct, quite correct, dear Thornton. You have an exceptionally acute financial brain. ... Right! With the recent loans to Hungary and Yugoslavia I was vulnerable to an attack from the naughty "bears", I know. Twenty-three percent off. ... yes, undoubtedly serious, dear boy, but what you don't know, and none of you know are two things. First, the Antonescu Foundation, of which as you know, my wife is President, is ready at any moment to make me a substantial loan. ... A charitable concern, of course, but a loan is perfectly legal, and don't you believe, dear old fellow, that charity begins at home? So that brings my immediately realizable assets to something in the nature of several hundred million dollars. ...

Carol (*watching Basil's body language from the kitchenette*) Don't worry. He seems confident.

Basil Of course he seems confident. You heard him — it's a crisis of confidence and liquidity. He explained liquidity. He didn't explain confidence.

Gregor (*into the telephone*) I have held it back for a very simple reason, dear chap — I don't want my enemies to know that I have it.

Basil He couldn't, because it's all done with mirrors. What conjuror is going to give away his tricks.

Carol Sure, I can see the conjuror ...

Towards the end of Gregor's telephone conversation, Carol comes into the living-room with a tray of coffee things. She puts the tray down on the table and pours Basil a cup, plainly knowing exactly how he likes it, creaming and sugaring it herself. She then makes her own

Gregor (*into the telephone*) It is a "*masse de manoeuvre*" that I intend to launch against them at the very crisis of the battle. ... A "*masse de manoeuvre*". It means a force in reserve. ... No, you are quite right. It is not a banking term, it is a military metaphor. ... (*To Sven*) Thornton must go. (*Into the telephone*) Now, second, and most important. The merger between Manson Radios and American Electric has not failed ... I repeat, *has not failed,* and will, after all, go through. Herries is meeting me here in fifteen minutes … Yes, it *will* go through. You have my word dearest Thornton! You have my word. Happier now? I am so glad. … Good. Now, dear Viscount, would you please read over to me my balance sheet of June the first 1934 of Manson Radios. … I have made a note from memory of the January figures and I would like to compare them. Begin, please.

Carol hands the coffee to Basil

Basil Look, your girlish intuition has led you astray. I don't worship him now ——
Carol You don't? Why?
Basil He's changed.
Gregor (*into the telephone*) There's no need to go slowly, Thornton, I'm *not* writing it down.
Carol How has he changed?
Basil Well — the system has changed him ——
Carol (*placidly sipping on her own cup of coffee*) Oh. The system.
Basil (*fiercely*) Yes. The system. The system does pervert and destroy human character. That's not just a slogan. It's the truth.
Gregor (*into the telephone*) I'm not writing it down, Thornton. Don't you know me well enough by now?
Basil When he was a child in Bucharest, he starved — I mean literally starved — his belly swollen from hunger, sitting in the gutter, begging for a crust of bread. His father drank and beat him. His mother hated him. He was the fifth child and they couldn't hope to feed four, let alone five. But he was the one who did the begging because at three or four his sores were so repulsive, and his face so thin, and his eyes so huge that people did sometimes press a coin into his hand — always being careful to look the other way ——
Carol How do you know all this?
Basil It's in all the biographies. You've only got to go to the public library.
Gregor (*into the phone*) Give me the undistributed profit again.
Carol (*placidly finishing her coffee*) I bet they didn't look the other way.
Basil What do you mean?
Carol I bet they chose him because he was the most persuasive. And the prettiest.

Basil turns his head away in exasperation

Gregor (*into the telephone*) Preferred ordinary interim, please, once more.
Carol (*irrepressible*) And I'm wondering about those sores. Can you be sure they weren't painted on?
Basil (*in genuine anguish*) Don't make a joke of it.

Carol (*going to him instantly*) Darling, I'm sorry. (*She embraces him*)
Gregor (*into the telephone*) That figure seems high.
Basil It's all right. It's only important to me to remember sometimes
  why ——
Carol Of course it is. That man in there is your business, not mine. You're
  my business and I didn't mean to hurt you. (*Looking at her watch*) I've got
  to get going. Darling, if there's anything I can do to help tonight ——
Basil Come back ...
Carol You're damn right I will ...
Gregor (*into the telephone*) Thank you, Thornton. ... Yes. I have all I need.
  Good-night. And sleep soundly, dear old fellow. (*He rings off. To Sven*)
  He's an idiot.
Carol (*kissing Basil on the mouth*) I do love you, you know. More than ever
  now, I think.
Basil I love you too. Whatever happens tonight, will you remember that?

*Gregor moves in to the living-room, followed by Sven. Basil breaks away
from Carol almost if he had been caught in a guilty act*

Gregor Goodness. I am sorry. You must please forgive me. (*To Sven*) This
  chair here, please, for me. Here — (*pointing*) is where Herries sits.

Sven, under his instructions, rearranges the furniture

  (*To Basil*) So if I understand correctly, you are going to marry this
  charming girl?
Carol (*boldly*) The subject has been broached, Mr Antonescu, but more by
  me than by your son. I must go. (*She begins to collect her things*)
Gregor Too bad. (*To Sven*) No. Not so close. About twelve inches more. (*To
  Basil*) But why not, dear boy? You've known each other how long?
Basil Six months.
Gregor (*to Sven*) Now that light out, I think. (*To Basil*) Six months? Well
  in these frank days I am quite sure that you have discovered all there is to
  know about each other.

Pause

Carol Yes, I think we have, Mr Antonescu. All there is to know.
Gregor So what is the impediment, dearest boy?
Carol I don't think he can answer that.
Gregor You can?
Carol I couldn't before this evening. Now I have a glimmering of an idea.
  Basil? (*She holds out her arms to Basil almost as if commanding him to
  come and kiss her in front of his father*)

This Basil does. Gregor abruptly turns to Sven

Gregor No, that is not right. That lamp over there for me.
Basil (*to Carol*) I'll walk you to the subway.
Gregor (*sharply*) No.
Basil Why not, father?
Gregor I want you here. You can help me.
Basil How?
Gregor By making yourself agreeable. Dearest boy, this is *your* apartment
— and so Mr Herries, the President of American Electric Incorporated, is,
strictly speaking, *your* guest. (*To Sven*) Put that light on please.

Sven does so. Gregor is now paying no attention to Carol and Basil

Basil (*kissing her*) See you after the show.
Carol Goodbye, Mr Antonescu.
Gregor Goodbye, — Miss — er ... (*To Sven*) That is much better, Sven.
Well done. Good-night, Miss Penn.
Carol Good-night.

Basil sees Carol to the door

Carol exits

Gregor (*looking at his watch*) Five minutes.

*As Basil moves back into the room he looks at him appraisingly with a slight
frown*

Dearest boy — would you do me a favour? Would you divest yourself of
that frightful dinner-jacket?
Basil (*self-consciously*) I know it must look terrible. I bought it for nine
dollars. Still, that's a lot for working clothes. (*He moves to the bedroom
door*) What shall I put on?
Gregor Have you a good suit?
Basil Nothing you would call good. I mean they are all over five years old
and hang on me a bit.
Gregor (*considering him*) Yes, they would. You're too thin. What do you
usually wear then?
Basil Down here in the Village, usually slacks and a sweater or shirt. Sandals,
too, I'm afraid
Gregor Something Bohemian, then. Well, Mr Herries is a snob but he is also
known to have literary leanings. I'm sure he would rather have written
Gray's Elegy than captured America — which financially speaking one
might say he almost has. May I come and advise?

Basil Yes, father.

Gregor leads the way into the bedroom

*Mark Herries, followed by David Beeston, come down the basement steps
and knock at the front door*

There he is.
Gregor (*unalarmed*) Two minutes early. (*Pulling down a pair of trousers*)
These are rather chic.

*Sven, in the living-room, is unhurriedly putting the coffee things in the kitchen
before going to the front-door — he too knows that Herries is early and
Gregor occupied*

Basil They're really for the beach.
Gregor They look expensive.
Basil They're not.
Gregor Looks are all that count. Now, where are your shirts?
Basil (*undressing*) Over there.

*There is another knock. Sven opens the door. Mark Herries, a smooth highly
prosperous-looking man in his fifties comes in. He is followed by David
Beeston, who looks like what he is, an accountant. He is in the middle thirties,
earnest and sincere. Also more than a little awed by the occasion. He carries
a briefcase*

Sven Good-evening, Mr Herries.
Herries Good-evening, Johnson.
Sven It's extremely good of you to come — I'm sure you understand that
this afternoon's appointment at the Antonescu Building was impossible in
view of the circumstances ——
Herries Even I have had to run from the reporters today — one of them got
into the Harvard Club tonight, he was turned out at once of course. Now,
I've brought Mr Beeston with me. He was our accountant who inspected
those books in Bucharest, and unearthed that little — discrepancy. Mr
Beeston, Mr Sven Johnson. The Crown Prince of the Antonescu empire.
(*To Sven*) You don't mind that appellation?
Sven I'm very flattered. But my succession, if it comes, is a very distant
prospect. Won't you sit down?

*Sven tries to manoeuvre Herries into his designated seat, but fails. Herries
takes another seat. Beeston remains standing*

Gregor (*in the bedroom where he has finally selected a rather brightly-coloured silk shirt*) This one, I think.

Sven Can I take your things? (*He puts away Herries' hat and gloves*)

Basil (*simultaneously*) Yes, that one was expensive, a present. But I've never worn it. It's too chi-chi for me.

Gregor Ah, no, not at all. It should suit you very well and go well with those slacks, too ——

Sven I think you'll find the sofa more comfortable.

Herries I'm very happy in this chair, thank you.

Sven I'll just tell G.A. you're here.

Herries How is he?

Sven (*moving to the bedroom*) You'll see for yourself in a moment. Excuse me.

Gregor Very smart.

Sven (*entering the bedroom and closing door behind him*) He's brought that accountant.

Gregor Good. That's what I hoped. (*To Basil*) Perhaps the hair needs a little attention.

Basil Yes, father. (*He moves into the shower*)

Herries (*to Beeston*) You have the statements and the accounts?

Beeston (*tapping his briefcase*) I have. Everything's in here.

Gregor (*quietly*) Our private information on Herries is correct, isn't it?

Sven His part in the Medworth deal?

Gregor No. Private information.

Sven Yes, I understand. (*Looking at Gregor admiringly*) Yes. That information — quite correct.

Gregor Anything concrete?

Sven Someone called …

Gregor (*with a hitherto unheard intensity*) Someone called what?

Herries And of course the press statement for nine o'clock?

Beeston Yes, Mr Herries.

Gregor (*to Sven*) What?

Herries Keep everything readily available. I know my adversary. You don't.

Gregor Remember! You must remember ——

Sven (*suddenly*) Larter. Mike Larter.

Gregor How old?

Sven Early twenties.

Gregor Recently?

Sven He died of an overdose last year.

Gregor Was Herries involved?

Sven Not directly. The inquest may have been fixed. But Larter had no job, left no money and it was an expensive apartment.

Gregor Where?

Sven Park Avenue, I think.
Gregor (*intensely*) Don't think. Be sure!

Basil comes out of the bathroom . He lies on the bed

  (*Instantly relaxes the tone of his voice*) So you can't be quite certain of that,
  Sven?
Sven Almost certain ——
Gregor Bravo. Very neat, very tidy. I think your father need a little sprucing
  up too.

Gregor moves into the bathroom

Herries Extraordinary place for G.A. to choose for a conference.
Gregor A little hot water under the eyes, I think. Three nights without sleep
  mustn't be shown ——
Herries Some kind of hideout, I suppose.
Beeston Yes, Mr Herries. It certainly looks like it.
Gregor Well, dear boy — now a rather decisive meeting, perhaps the most
  decisive of my life. (*He smiles*) As a good socialist, I know you must hope
  it fails. As my son, it would help me to have your blessing.
Basil You have my blessing, father.
Herries Peculiar, most peculiar. I'm afraid it does look a little — doesn't it,
  Beeston?— like a cornered rat.
Gregor Thank you. Come in only when I open the door. Oh — and better
  not call me father. Our friend is a little — straight-laced about wedlock.
Basil Yes, father.
Gregor So you remain Basil Anthony. Right?
Basil Right.
Gregor (*to Sven*) Stay facing the accountant.
Sven I'd better warn you, G.A, Herries is sitting in your chair.
Gregor Trust him. (*He moves into the living-room, followed by Sven*) My
  dear Mark, how very good of you to come to my little downtown dump,
  and at such an hour.
Herries (*rising*) Oh, it's not a dump, G.A. It's a very unusual and decorative
  little hideout.
Gregor (*smiling*) Not exactly a hideout, Mark. If I should ever in the future,
  have need of such a thing, I have better ones than this, I assure you. No, this
  is just a little — place I — use from time to time. Do sit down. (*He indicates
  the intended seat*)

Herries has no option but to take the indicated place. Gregor sits in the chair he intended for himself

You understand why I had to postpone our earlier meeting?

Herries You've been pretty well hounded today, I should imagine.

Gregor (*with an amused shrug*) Twenty-three percent off the value of all my shares in one day has apparently made the press photographers even more anxious to get close up photographs of my dull face.

Herries I'm so sorry, G.A. ——

Gregor (*interrupting hastily*) Dear Mark — these things happen. (*With a smile*) Not perhaps to American Electric — but anyway to me. I'm not a solid and respectable president of a vast, solid and respectable corporation like you. I'm a speculator — and known to be. So — when a vague rumour hits Wall Street that a merger has failed ——

Herries (*grimly*) Hardly a rumour, G.A. Our merger has failed. And Beeston and I are here tonight, I'm afraid, to tell you so. (*Looking at Beeston*) Oh, forgive me. May I introduce —— ?

Gregor (*raising his hand politely to stop Herries*) Just one moment. (*Nodding at Beeston, the first time he has looked at him*) Forgive me, dear fellow. (*To Herries*) Just — as they say over here, for the record — a rumour is still a rumour even if, as in this case, it tells the truth.

Herries I stand corrected. Now, this is Mr Beeston.

Gregor gets up to greet Beeston, who rises and shakes hands nervously

Gregor Good of you to come.

Beeston Not at all, Mr Antonescu.

Herries Beeston is the accountant who ——

Gregor (*amiably, as he resumes his seat*) Ah. The villain of the piece.

Herries (*smiling*) Yes. The villain of the piece.

Gregor (*smiling at Beeston*) I am very happy to meet a young man whose command of figures and understanding of balance sheets can wreck a great merger and cause a full-scale panic on Wall Street. Do either of you smoke?

Herries No, G.A.

Gregor Just as well, perhaps. I doubt if this "dump" — as you called it — holds any cigarettes. Certainly no cigars.

Herries I don't think I called it a dump, G.A. I think you did.

Gregor (*shrugging*) Does it matter who called it what? It is a dump, and it has no cigarettes or cigars. It doesn't — as you may have guessed — belong to me.

Herries I didn't really think so. Who does it belong to?

Gregor Well, shall we get to business.

Herries (*hit on his sensitive Harvard Club solar plexus*) I'm sorry. By all means. Beeston, will you hand Mr Antonescu a copy of the statement we propose to issue this evening.

Gregor Would you read it out, please? You very young people are so lucky in possessing eyes that don't need glasses ——
Beeston I'm not *very* young, Mr Antonescu.

Gregor waves him to read

(*Reading*) "The President of the Board of American Electric Incorporated announce that the projected merger of certain of their interests with Manson Radios will not now take place."
Gregor It sounds a little as if you and I had a tiff at the alter, Mark.
Herries (*enjoying the joke*) I rather agree. (*To Beeston*) Would you reword it to sound a little less like a broken engagement?
Beeston I could say — "has collapsed" ——
Gregor (*amused*) "Collapsed" is perhaps not the most fortunate of terms to apply to a concern of mine at this precise moment in world history. You have read tonight's newspapers, Mr — er ...
Sven (*prompting*) Beeston.
Gregor I'm so sorry. Surely a name of all names I should remember. (*To Herries*) No doubt when I die you will find Beeston engraved on my heart. How is it spelt? B E A S T?
Herries (*smiling; he does not much like Beeston either*) No. B double E, I'm afraid.
Gregor A pity. (*To Beeston*) I'm so sorry, dear fellow. A very poor joke. Please go on.
Beeston Shall I say "has failed"?
Gregor (*after a pause*) I think perhaps you should leave the precise phrasing to Mr Herries. I'm sure you'll find a Harvard education adequate to the task. Please read from there.
Beeston (*muttering*) "Not now take place" ——
Gregor Yes, that's right from there.
Beeston "Information received ... "
Gregor What immortal phrase have you found to describe the cause of my ruptured romance with Mr Herries?
Beeston (*ploughing ahead bravely*) "Information received by the President and Board following the visit to Bucharest of Mr David Beeston, account of the ——
Gregor (*bowing to Beeston*) Quite right. Credit where credit is due — young fellow ——
Herries (*impatiently with Beeston*) Just say — "of one of the corporation's accountants" — it's quite enough.
Beeston (*making a correction*) Yes, Mr Herrie. " —visit to Bucharest of one of the corporation's accountants have convinced them" (*To Gregor*) That's the President and Board ——

Gregor (*with a shade of impatience*) I had gathered that, Mr Beeston.

Beeston (*doggedly, but growing a little shrill*) "Convinced them that the state of finances of certain of the foreign subsidiaries of Manson Radios"
——

Gregor (*to Herries*) Rather a lot of "ofs" there. (*To Beeston*) It doesn't matter at all, my dear fellow. Mr Herries and I can work on the syntax later. (*He waves him on*)

Beeston is becoming angry and this is exactly what Gregor wants

Beeston (*angrily*) Can I just give you the sense, Mr Antonescu, and forget the syntax?

Gregor (*after a quick eyebrow raising at Herries*) Dear fellow — your sense has been painfully clear to me ever since Mr Herries informed me last week that you seemed to have discovered some flaw in our accounting ——

Beeston (*hotly*) Flaw seems to me a pretty mild word for what I found over there ——

Gregor Did you enjoy Bucharest?

Beeston I didn't have much time to enjoy anything, Mr Antonescu — and what I discovered in your books ——

Gregor Surely Pavlovski showed you some of the pleasures of my birthplace? I hope he took you to one particular little joint — my favourite
——

Beeston Pavlovski? Who's Pavlovski?

Gregor Our chief accountant.

Beeston I spent all my time with a guy called Andreiev — he showed me the books. He didn't say he wasn't chief ——

Gregor (*to Sven*) Andreiev? Who is he?

Sven One of the pool of accountants.

Gregor I hadn't heard of him. It was this ——

Sven (*prompting*) Andreiev ——

Gregor — Andreiev who looked after you in Bucharest? Sven, should a minor accountant have been given so important an assignment?

Sven (*humbly*) I'm very sorry, G.A. It was my mistake. Pavlovski was on holiday and so were both his assistants. I had no idea that Mr — Beeston here wished to make so full an examination. I thought he was merely looking for information on certain minor matters relating to the merger. Andreiev seemed perfectly competent for that ——

Beeston But these discrepancies I found *were* relating to the merger. After all — an entry on Manson's Roumanian subsidiary listed as "cash in hand and in banks" and amounting to over twelve million dollars ——

Gregor (*very quietly*) Eleven million, three hundred and seventy-six thousand, nine hundred ——

Beeston Well, I have the figure here. (*He pulls out a document and reads*) "Eleven million three hundred and seventy-six thousand, nine hundred. (*Confused*) I was speaking from memory.

Herries So was Mr Antonescu.

Gregor (*politely*) You were saying?

Beeston (*flustered and angry*) An item — whatever the exact amount — listed here as "Cash in hand and in banks" – turns out, on examination in Bucharest to be "Cash, bankings and on deposit" — that is the literal translation from the Roumanian ——

Gregor *Felicitari pentu Romanineasca Dumneavoastra excelenta.*

Beeston I beg your pardon?

Gregor I'm sorry. What I said was — congratulations on your excellent Roumanian.

Beeston (*now really heated*) Listen, Mr Antonescu — I didn't need to learn Roumanian. Figures are the same in any language.

Gregor Of course. Not necessarily the methods of accounting ——

Beeston (*loudly*) The amount you told Mr Herries and his board here as standing to the credit of Manson Radios Roumanian subsidiary is short by six million dollars. OK. Go on. Tell me the exact figure down to the last cent. I've heard of that trick and it's a great one, and I'm sure it's impressed a lot of people in your time — but six million dollars is a mighty large error in bookkeeping — and you don't get me — in front of Mr Herries — to ——

Gregor (*tapping his knee gently to stop the flood*) Dear fellow, dear fellow, dear fellow. How you do go on. I was only going to ask if either of you would like a little refreshment. (*To Herries*) I'm afraid there is only bourbon and gin — which is all the young man keeps here — would you care —— ?

Herries No, thank you. Perhaps Beeston —— ?

Gregor You think it might loosen his tongue perhaps? Mr Beeston?

Beeston No, thank you. I'm sorry, Mr Antonescu. You must please forgive me — I had no right to speak that way.

Gregor But my dear fellow, anyone who has caused a major world financial crisis — off his own — bat — isn't that the expression? — Has surely the right to be a little — tetchy. Dear Mr Beeston, I am here to be questioned. You are here to question me. So question me.

Beeston Well, Mr Antonescu, these six million dollars I found listed on your balance sheet as on deposit, I later discovered after a very difficult investigation, had, in fact, been debited to Antonescu Holdings — and the collateral ——

Gregor (*to Sven*) Does this — Andreiev — does he speak English?

Sven Hardly at all.

Gregor That explains a great deal.

Beeston (*growing angry again*) Andreiev could make himself understood well enough ——

Gregor And if he couldn't, the figures could, eh? Even though the words beside them were written in Roumanian ——

Beeston OK. So I don't speak Roumanian. We settled that, didn't we? But figures are the same in any language. We settled that too. Here they are, Mr Antonescu. I suggest you look at them.

Gregor (*to Herries*) The owner has Bohemian taste, don't you think?

Herries Well, it's — interesting.

Gregor In certain matters one occasionally has to be a little — indulgent. You agree?

Herries (*interested and puzzled, but uncomfortable*) Sure.

Gregor Besides, the Village is not exactly — Park Avenue, is it, Mark?

Herries (*stiffly*) No.

Gregor That was a very different apartment.

Herries Whose apartment?

Gregor (*lightly*) Mike Larter's. (*To Beeston*). I'm so sorry, Mr Beeston, I interrupted you. You wanted me to look at some figures, didn't you?

Herries May I change my mind, G.A.?

Gregor (*deep in the document*) Of course. (*With a wave*) Sven ——

Sven moves to the kitchenette

Sven I don't know where the young man keeps his ice. (*Finding some ice*) Ah, yes.

Herries (*murmuring*) You don't know this apartment, Johnson?

Sven (*murmuring back, with a faintly suggestive smile*) Of its existence, yes. I'm the only one. But even I have never been invited inside before. You and I are very privileged. Of course, it is a rather special occasion tonight. (*Raising his voice a fraction, so as to carry to Gregor*) It's the young owner-occupier's birthday. I don't know much — I'm not allowed to — but I do know where G.A. can invariably be reached on the evening on July thirteenth.

Beeston (*prodding the document with his finger*) There it is, Mr Antonescu! There! In black and white. And not in Roumanian either. Six million dollars listed as cash in hand — actually debited to Antonescu Holdings. Explain *that* away if you can.

Herries Beeston — please! Do try and remember your manners.

Beeston I'm sorry, Mr Herries. But a deficiency of six million dollars is ——

Herries A deficiency of six million dollars. I know. But there are ways of expressing these things.

Gregor It's actually a surplus of one million dollars, but Mr Beeston could hardly be expected to see that ——

Herries How, G.A.?

Gregor The six million on loan to Antonescu Holdings has been used to buy
up a radio concern in France — I think I told you the other day — or did
I forget?

Herries No. You told me. But I had had a rough meeting with the Board.
They were furious about Beeston's bombshell. I wasn't perhaps listening
with as much concentration as I should. On what collateral is the loan
secured?

Gregor Italian bonds worth, at present valuation, seven million five hundred
and seventy thousand ——

Beeston (*frantically searching among his documents*) Wait a minute. Wait
a minute. Those are not at all my figures.

Gregor (*ignoring him totally*) So I should have said a profit of a million and
a half. But I am, as you know, rather conservative about estimated profits
— I believe I'll join you in a bourbon, Mark.

Sven Not much left.

Gregor Rather looks as if *carissimo* has been punishing it a little. Ah, well.
On anniversaries all things are permitted.

*Beeston is still frantically searching his documents. The others totally ignore
him*

Herries (*murmuring*) I had heard this was rather a special occasion ——

Gregor Sven, that was naughty of you.

Sven I'm sorry.

Gregor There are certain things we all like to keep dark. Some things darker
than others. It's not for nothing I've got the press title "mystery man".
Actually Mark — you're something of a mystery man yourself. You know
— if it hadn't been for that evening I was taken to that apartment ——

Herries I'd no idea you knew Mike Larter. No idea at all.

Gregor Oh, I hardly did know him, Mark. I would have liked to know him
very well indeed, but — (*His shrug is quietly suggestive of Herries'
proprietorial rights*)

Herries But Mike would have told me ——

Gregor I went as Mr Gregory. Not very original.

Herries Who brought you?

Gregor Oh, a young friend. I forget his name. What a tragic business that
was about Mike ——

Herries (*quickly*) It was an accident, you know ——

Gregor Oh, of course ——

Herries The foolish boy would take those damnable pills. I couldn't stop him
— and then the drink as well ——

Gregor My dear Mark, I felt for you most deeply at the time, I couldn't of
course, tell you.

Beeston (*with a triumphant shout*) I've got it! I'm so sorry, Mr Herries. May I interrupt?

Herries Yes? What is it, Beeston?

Beeston The real value of the Italian Bonds used by Mr Antonescu as collateral for his loan to his own company is, according to our reckoning — four million, seven hundred thousand, five hundred and so that leaves a deficit of ——

Gregor (*with amusement*) You got those figures from the Wall Street Journal! Dear boy. Do me a favour. And I think Mr Herries a favour — because this merger would not have been wholly unprofitable to American Electric. Go home and put through a long distance call to the Finance Minister in Mussolini's government. Just ask him at what price he values these bonds, as of this moment. (*Pleased to have remembered the phrase so aptly*) As of this moment, dear boy. Do that and tell Mr Herries the result tomorrow. It won't affect the deal which you have killed. But I think the Minister's reply will interest Mr Herries and the Board. (*To Herries*) Mark, have another. (*To Sven*) Sven, remind me to send the boy a case of bourbon tomorrow ——

Beeston Listen — you know damn well I've as much chance of getting through on the telephone to the Italian Finance Minister — as I have of getting through to Signor Mussolini ——

Gregor (*gently*) But you could very easily get through to Signor Mussolini if you cared to use my name ——

Herries Why don't you do just that, Beeston?

Beeston (*finally speechless*) Jesus!

Herries (*sternly*) What did you say, Beeston?

Beeston You'd better take over, Mr Herries. I can see there's nothing more I can do here ——

Herries Don't be hysterical man! It happens to be true that Mr Antonescu's name will get you access to almost any Head of State in Europe.

Gregor Are you leaving out the White House, Mark?

Herries Yes, I hear he consults you now and then. (*Smiling*) Don't care much for some of the advice you seem to have been giving him ——

Gregor (*shrugging, smiling*) Desperate times demand desperate remedies ——

Beeston I guess I'm a little out of my depth here. All I know is — because it's my job to know it — and because you pay me good money to find it out, and because I'm a loyal servant of American Electric ——

Herries Whoever said you weren't?

Gregor Your loyalty, Mr Beeston, is the sole quality of yours that none of us have ever questioned.

Beeston Jesus!

Herries I wish you wouldn't use that particular expletive, Beeston. It's not very seemly on an occasion like this. But go on. All you know is —— ?

Beeston That this here — (*pointing at Gregor*) has tried to snitch six million dollars from American Electric, and falsified his books in Bucharest to cover it up ——

Sven laughs on cue. Herries is much amused

Gregor (*to Herries*) Snitch? (*To Sven*) Please remember that for me, would you? Snitch.

Herries (*very seriously to Beeston*) I'm afraid I think you *had* better go, Beeston.

Beeston Jesus! I told you — I'm — (*he remembers who his boss is*) I've already told you, Mr Herries, I'm going.

Gregor You won't have a nightcap, dear fellow? Sven ——

Sven (*to Beeston*) Oh — perhaps you had better leave behind that copy of the press statement — the one Mr Herries and Mr Antonescu were going to alter the syntax of a little — thank you so much. Good-night.

Beeston exits

Gregor (*calling*) Good-night, dear fellow. Isn't he very young to be your chief accountant, Mark?

Herries Well — as it happens — he's not actually our *chief* accountant. But he's a good, bright boy, G.A. ——

Gregor Plainly as bright as a button. The only cause I have for wonder — forgive me dear fellow — is how you came to entrust this particular bright boy with the whole future of world finance?

Herries Isn't that putting it a big high, G.A.?

Gregor (*indifferently*) I don't think so, Mark. You saw what the mere mention of our merger's failure did to Wall Street today. When that — (*he points to Beeston's statement*) — is published tomorrow my whole group could easily be wiped out. (*Chuckling amiably*) In fact, I've already told Sven here that in a few more weeks I fully expect to be left with nothing more than a few houses, office buildings, furniture, pictures and a couple of oil wells at Ploesti ——

Herries Well, G.A., it's good to know that whatever else happens, your personal fortune won't be affected ——

Gregor My personal fortune? How much is it? I don't know. It's the one figure I've never bothered to count or remember. Three or four million — perhaps a little more — but quite insufficient, for instance, to help the Austrians defeat the new run on their currency as I had promised Dolfuss ——

Herries You shouldn't promise, G.A. Your trouble is simple. You've spread yourself out too wide — far too wide, G.A. ——
Gregor (*suddenly with fervent intensity*) Of course I have. And why? Because I'm a fighter and I know my enemy. So do you. Liquidity and confidence, that's all the crisis is about. What else have I fought for all my life? Who gave roads to Yugoslavia and electricity to Hungary? And what will the unemployment figure reach in America when my group crashes? (*Mildly after a sigh*) Yes, Mark, I've spread myself out too wide.
Herries Well, I have always admired your courage — but there is, in my view, a basic unsoundness in inflationary financing ——
Gregor Yes, yes, yes. Dear Mark, don't let's argue finance. (*Pointing to the document*) My battle is over and lost anyway. No point in wasting breath. Now – I think it's time you met our host. (*He opens the door to the bedroom and calls*) Carissimo. You can come out now. Our business is finished.

Basil gets up from the bed and walks into the living-room. Herries looks at Basil

I want you to meet a very good friend of mine, called Mark. Mark, this is Basil. Not too bored waiting, I hope?
Basil No, I thought you'd be much longer. I thought business conferences always went on all night.
Gregor Some do. But not this one. The issue has been decided against me before it began. I was given no chance to fight.
Herries That's a little unfair, G.A.
Gregor (*laying his hand on Basil's shoulder; with a smile*) Well, then — give me a chance to fight. Let me come to your Board tomorrow and explain this mysterious sum that I've tried to — (*he stops and clicks his fingers*) Sven?
Sven Snitch.
Gregor Snitch from American Electric ——
Herries (*sincerely*) G.A., I'm sorry about that. Really sorry. I guess Beeston just lost his head, that's all. And yet he's supposed to be a level-headed enough young man.
Gregor Is he? (*Bitterly*) I'm glad I haven't got a head so level that it can throw another million or more out of work because of a minor confusion between American and Roumanian banking practices. (*To Basil; whom he is gently holding*) Do you approve of that sort of level-head, dear boy?
Basil No. Certainly not.
Gregor (*fondly; to Herries*) Basil has a strong social conscience. (*To Basil*) I like the shirt. Is it in honour of Mr Herries?
Basil Yes. In your honour, too.

Gregor (*releasing Basil and moving away*) I'm flattered. I hope you are, Mark.

Herries Very honoured indeed. Where did you get it?

Basil A present ——

Herries (*looking at Gregor*) Ah, I see. It suits you, if I may borrow an expression from our English cousins, a fair treat. You *are* English, aren't you?

Basil No. Just brought up there.

Gregor He's a hundred percent, red-blooded American boy, Mark. Don't let his Oxford accent fool you.

Herries (*his snob instincts now aroused*) Oxford, eh? Which college?

Basil Christ Church.

Herries The "House". Isn't that what it's called?

Basil Yes. By some people.

Herries I don't know about your social conscience, but I notice you chose yourself a pretty "posh" college there.

Gregor (*quietly*) Perhaps the choice wasn't entirely his own.

Herries Ah. (*To Basil*) Gee, Basil — I almost forgot to wish you many happy returns.

Gregor You don't think it's his *birthday*, do you, Mark? Even Basil has only one birthday a year — March the twelfth — right, Basil?

Basil Yes.

Gregor There are things I keep even from Sven — for instance, the very special significance of this date.

Herries (*puzzled*) But G.A., you said ——

Gregor I said "anniversary". I don't think we'd better go on about it, Mark, or we'll embarrass poor Basil. *Carissimo*, we seem to have polished off your whisky. I'm so sorry. Would you be an angel and get me another bottle? Just a moment, dear boy.

Basil pauses. Gregor turns to Sven with a quick gesture to his breast pocket. Sven slips out his wallet and hands a ten dollar bill to Gregor, who gives it to Basil. Basil holds the bill, looking at his father with troubled enquiry and still not able to believe his mounting suspicions. There is no answer for him in Gregor's eyes. They are quite expressionless and blank

Basil turns to the door and exits

Herries Well, well, well.

Gregor Poor dear Basil. Always so shy with strangers. Especially, of course, with the famous Mark Herries ——

Herries I wonder — G.A. — I wonder if ... (*He glances at Sven*)

Gregor Sven, be a good fellow, and leave us alone a moment.

*Sven nods and goes into the bedroom. There is a pause after he has gone.
Herries is longing to ask a lot of questions, but Gregor is determined not to
help him too much. He patiently awaits the first question*

Herries G.A. — I'm sorry I can't phrase it any better than this — forgive the
bluntness — but — is — well, is — what I am thinking true?
Gregor Dear Mark — always so direct. How do I know what you are
thinking? That Basil's my son?
Herries No, no, although you did have a son, didn't you? I remember you
telling me he died five years ago.

Gregor nods

Very sad for you. No, I wasn't thinking quite of a son … (*He flounders into
silence*)
Gregor (*touching his shoulder fondly*) Dear, dear Mark — let me put you
out of your doubts and suspicions at once. I asked you here because you are
one of the very few men in New York I would trust with the truth. (*Simply*)
So now you have the truth.
Herries I'm staggered G.A. Absolutely staggered. Jesus! (*catching himself
up*) — but G.A. — those mistresses, you have the most highly publicized
mistresses of any man in the world — also a very fascinating wife — come
to think of it — even more publicized ——
Gregor Dear Mark, what is for public show is not always for private
pleasure. About Beeston — could I ask you a favour?
Herries (*absently*) Sure.
Gregor When I come tomorrow to meet your Board and explain this — I've
forgotten the word again — ah, yes — "snitching" — could I, please, be
spared the presence of Mr Beeston?
Herries Well, most unhappily, Beeston is the man who personally inspected
those books. He's the only one with all the relevant facts. I really think we
ought to have him there.
Gregor (*with a wide gesture*) Then I don't come. I'm sorry, Mark. I just don't
come.
Herries I'll get him to apologize to you personally ——
Gregor No, no, I'm sorry, Mark. It's not just that word, for heaven's sake.
It's not the first time I've had criminal slanders of that kind flung at my
head. I've always laughed at them, you know that. (*Suddenly intensely
serious*) It's *hysteria*, Mark — in matters of high finance I hate dealing with
hysterics ——
Herries Beeston? Before tonight there's never been a sign ——
Gregor Dear Mark, the indications are obvious. Those eyes. Haven't you
ever noticed the pupils?

Herries No, I can't say I have. You can't mean you think he takes drugs?

Gregor I don't mean anything, Mark. I am sure you have checked up on his private life. (*Firmly*) I just mean I can't stand hysterics.

Herries All right. I'll get Broadbent. He's senior and I expect he'll be briefed on the facts. But tomorrow? Did we say tomorrow?

Gregor That's what I thought *you* said.

Herries But, G.A. — I can't convene my whole board by tomorrow.

Gregor (*with a smile*) And of course you never make any decision without a board, do you, Mark? (*Carelessly*) Make it Wednesday then, and I'll bring my board too - if that's how you want it — (*He shrugs and looks at a picture*) The boy is developing quite a taste for pictures, I'm glad to see ——

Herries If we meet alone I'll need *two* accountants.

Gregor After what happened tonight I think that might be advisable.

Herries You can bring two of yours.

Gregor Thank you. I'll come alone.

Herries (*nodding resignedly*) What time tomorrow? Would three p.m. suit?

Gregor Admirably. (*He picks up the statement from the table and, smiling at Herries, tears it up slowly and drops the pieces into the waste-paper basket*)

Herries (*smiling*) Don't count your chickens, G.A.

Gregor I never do. (*Looking at the picture again*) Do you know Mark, I'm so pleased I seem to be teaching him something. I'm able to see so very little of him. He gets lonely, I'm afraid. It would be very good of you, Mark, when I'm in Europe, if sometime, perhaps ——

Herries I'd be delighted, G.A. Delighted.

Gregor (*carelessly*) Oh, I wish I hadn't torn up that statement.

Herries Why?

Gregor Well, the press have been told to expect a statement and after what happened on Wall Street today I think we have to say something. (*Calling*) Sven ——

Herries Well, it's difficult to know just what to say.

Gregor How about this? Sven, would you take this down please.

Sven nods and whips out a notebook

"Mr Mark Herries — President of American Electric Incorporated —" (*genially*) — We'll leave out your board this time, shall we, Mark?

Basil enters with a bottle of bourbon

Ah. Good boy. Pour out a drink for Mr Herries, would you?

Herries (*looking at Basil*) Just a very small one ——

Basil nods and goes to the drinks trolley

Gregor (*to Sven*) "Mr Mark Herries etc. wishes to state that the rumours at present circulating Wall Street regarding the failure of the projected merger with Manson Radios Incorporated have no foundation whatever in fact ——"

Basil turns, startled

Herries (*startled*) Now listen — that's equivalent of saying the merger is going through. You must use your own phrase — "as of this moment—"
Gregor (*smoothly*) And that's the equivalent of saying the merger is not going through. No, wait. Let's just add this. "Negotiations are still actively proceeding between the respective heads of the two concerns, and it is confidently expected that a result will be reached tomorrow when a further statement will be issued." That's vague enough for you, isn't it, Mark?
Herries It seems to meet the case, G.A.
Gregor (*nodding to Sven peremptorily*) Good.

Sven moves into the bedroom. Once inside with the door closed he runs for the telephone and feverishly dials a number. This speech, from time to time inaudible, plays under the continuing action in the living-room

Sven (*in the bedroom, murmuring urgently*) William? — get this down ... For God's sake, man, don't waste time — every second is vital. Right. Are you ready? "Mr Mark Herries, President of American Electric Incorporated, wishes to state that the rumours at present circulating Wall Street regarding the failure of the projected merger with Manson Radios Incorporated have no foundation whatever in fact. Negotiations are still actively proceeding between the respective heads of the two concerns, and it is confidently expected that a conclusive result" — wait, William — omit conclusive — insert favourable. ... favourable result. ... No, but my memory isn't so good these days. Get me?. ... I agree. Conclusive could mean favourable, but favourable *does* mean favourable. No. He won't remember. If he does, it's my fault, not "The Man's". All right, William? Ready to go on — "favourable result will be reached today — July fourteenth — when a further statement will be issued." ... All right. Got it? Read it over. ... Yes, William. ... Yes, William. Back on top of the world. Control your exuberance a little would you, dear fellow, and read me the statement over?

Meanwhile, Herries has turned to Basil, visibly (but not obviously) exuding well-bred charm

Herries Basil — I may call you that, mayn't I? — I just did — and it isn't
too rude a question — have you an occupation of any kind? I know, of
course, you don't need ——

Basil (*in a strained voice*) I play the piano in a club on Twelfth Street.

Herries Really? Was it there you met … ? (*He nods at Gregor*)

Basil does not reply. Herries chuckles

Discretion. Good boy. You've plainly learnt some valuable lessons from
the mystery man of Europe.

Basil Yes.

Herries You must be proud — very proud — to have such a great man as
your particular friend.

Gregor (*quickly, his back still to them*) Don't flatter me too much, Mark.
Basil won't like it. Remember his social conscience.

Herries (*chuckling*) I've made that note, G.A. (*To Basil*) What is the name
of this club?

Basil (*at length*) The Green Hat.

Herries (*noting it down*) The Green Hat. On Twelfth Street. Thank you. (*Still
writing*) Basil — what is the surname?

Basil (*murmuring*) Anthony.

Herries (*writing*) Basil Anthony. Telephone?

Basil Gramercy 73961.

Herries Good. (*He closes his notebook*) I'll call you, if I may, after G.A. has
gone to Europe? Here is my card. We might fix an evening? Well.
Goodbye, G.A. Three p.m. tomorrow?

Gregor You surrounded with accountants. I, poor little lost boy, all alone to
face my accusers … (*Hint of steel*) Couldn't you do with *one* less
accountant, Mark?

Herries Well. Maybe. Just Broadbent, eh?

Gregor Broadbent's a very sound man. I get on very well with Broadbent.

Herries (*genially*) Sure. That's what I'm afraid of. (*Holding out his hand*)
OK. It's a promise. Thanks, G.A. My hat …

Gregor (*giving Basil a friendly push*) Basil, see your honoured guest out.

Herries It's been a great occasion.

Gregor Got your car, Mark?

Herries Yes, good-night, G.A.

Gregor Good-night.

Basil opens the door

Herries (*of the door*) Oh, how very kind of you, dear boy ——

Basil and Herries exit

Gregor Pleasant dreams.

Sven comes in to the living-room

Sven Man! Man! Never in your whole life ——
Gregor Don't say a word ...

They embrace, laughing

> I deserve it all. Oh, my God — (*he falls, utterly exhausted, on to the sofa*)
> I didn't know how tired I was. One more second of that silly, pink faced
> old — what is the American expression for it, Sven? — there is one very
> expressive one — not the English one ...

Sven shakes his head. Gregor closes his eyes

> You fail sometimes, Sven, you fail me. I've got it — fairy! That silly pink
> faced old fairy ——

*Basil enters. He runs into the bathroom, tearing off his shirt, and slams the
door*

> (*Sleepily*) What was that?
Sven Vassily ...
Gregor (*sleepily*) Keep an eye on him, Sven.
Sven (*goes into bedroom and knocks on bathroom door*) Vassily? Vassily?
  (*He comes back into the living- room*) He's locked himself in.
Gregor (*at length*) Of course. (*Making a huge effort to rouse himself*) Get
  to work. To all confidential centres the news that the merger is through ——
Sven Is it safe?
Gregor Safe? Care to bet some part of that million dollars you "snitched"
  — from the Polish deal and keep tucked away in the Guaranty Trust?
Sven (*after a pause*) No.
Gregor I thought not. Dear Sven, has there ever been anything safer? My
  crisis is over as of this moment. That curious little girl. Not unattractive
  though. I wonder why she wants to marry Vassily of all people? Oh, well.

Basil comes out of the bathroom. He is wearing a sweatshirt

> Now where was I? Yes. All centres. This message ——

*Basil moves in to the living-room. He stands facing his father, who returns
his gaze while still talking to Sven*

The merger will go through tomorrow and thus realize for my immediate use the cash sum of seventy-five million dollars. The crisis is therefore past. All payments can and will be met. There is no longer any single Antonescu enterprise anywhere in the world in any danger at all. To all my stockmarket agents just one word: "buy". Add another phrase — "And keep on buying". (*Still looking unwaveringly at Basil*) And Sven — I'm not boastful, as you know, but think it might not be bad for morale to preface all messages with some reference to me — by my code name of course. Perhaps: "The Man is still the Man". Do you like that?

Sven Excellent.

Gregor My dear Vassily, you were absolutely perfect. I'm sorry I had to pass you off as *un petit pederaste* in front of Mr Herries — but I had no choice. I hope you are not too cross with me.

Basil (*at length, with quiet intensity*) You are *nothing*. You live and breathe and have being and you are my father — but you are *nothing*.

Gregor does not reply. He stares up amusedly at his son

Basil turns and quickly runs out of the front door, slamming it after him

ACT II

Basil Anthony's basement apartment. The action is continuous

Sven and Gregor remain exactly as they were at the end of ACT I

Sven I'm going after him.
Gregor Why?
Sven Because it's too dangerous to let him roam around New York in that mood. It's too dangerous, G.A.
Gregor He can do no harm.
Sven He can talk.
Gregor (*relaxing again*) He won't.
Sven A word from him to Herries could kill the deal. If there's one thing the Herries type hates it's being made a fool of ——
Gregor (*murmuring sleepily*) There won't *be* a word from Vassily.
Sven You can't be sure.
Gregor (*sleepily*) I can. He had his chance to finish me five years ago. He didn't take it then. He won't take it now. In this world there are those who do and those who don't, Sven. Call them the strong and the weak, if you like. By now you should know on which side dear Vassily lies.
Sven (*after a pause*) What did he know, five years ago?
Gregor (*pause*) Too much.
Sven Why did you tell him too much?
Gregor He was my son. I told him everything. Why not? I showed him my secret balance sheet of the Antonescu Holdings. Everything.
Sven But G.A. — to a son who hated you.
Gregor Oh, dear Sven, how stupid you can be sometimes. (*He struggles into a sitting position*) I mustn't sleep. I must take two more of those pills.

Sven takes out a bottle, shakes two pills into his palm and hands them to Gregor reluctantly

Sven Too many of these are dangerous.
Gregor Any more dangerous than letting Vassily wander round New York with Mark Herries' private number in his pocket? Vassily won't harm me and nor will these pills.
Sven How was I stupid? I think you forget I once saw him try to kill you.

Gregor On the night he left me? Dear, dear Sven. One bullet in a chandelier six feet over my head doesn't argue a very serious attempt to kill. But — even suppose the bullet had been meant for my heart — what on earth has killing to do with hatred?

Pause. Sven shrugs

Sven You used to do your best to *make* him hate you.
Gregor Did I? Yes, I suppose I did.
Sven And tonight, too.
Gregor Tonight? (*He shrugs*) Perhaps. But if so it was unconscious. Vassily was useful to me tonight. That was all, I think.
Sven Well, you certainly took a big risk not to warn him of the part he was supposed to play.
Gregor I know I did, I had to. A far bigger risk than handing him that revolver five years ago and daring him to shoot me. (*With relish*) But Sven, how much more fun! (*He rises and moves around*) What I did tonight I did alone — without an accomplice — and that was important to me. A moment ago I asked you to boost my subordinates' morale. What about my own? Do you think I've enjoyed being on the run all day, sitting on a park bench in Washington Square with my coat collar turned up, thinking of Kreuger lying on that bed in Paris with that little hole through his heart, thinking of Loewenstein jumping from that plane? (*As an afterthought*) By the way — there's an interesting idea I had for a development in Washington Square. Remind me of it sometime, would you? (*He is striding around the room with gusto*)
Sven Why did you try to make Vassily hate you?

Pause. Gregor suddenly puts his hand to his head, as though bewildered

Gregor You change the subject rather quickly, Sven. We were talking about me — weren't we?
Sven Before we were talking about Vassily.
Gregor (*holding his head*) Why did I try to get Vassily to hate me? That was your question, wasn't it?
Sven Don't answer me if you don't want to.
Gregor (*angrily*) I'll answer any questions put to me by anyone in the world. (*He continues to hold his head*) These pills are working too fast, or something worse is happening. I'm losing concentration.

Sven is instantly by Gregor's side

Sven G.A. — you should sleep on that bed for at least two hours ——

Gregor (*pushing Sven away; panicky*) I'm not sleepy. But I mustn't lose concentration — God — if that happened — let me think of that balance sheet. (*He sits down; after a pause*) Yes. All right. (*With a normal voice after the panic*) The point is, of course, I have never been able to think very clearly about Vassily. After three nights of no sleep it makes it no easier ——

Sven Don't bother about Vassily ——

Gregor No. You asked me a question and I must answer it. Try to, at least. (*Pause*) I think I could have endured a daughter loving me — yes. A girl might have been different. (*Pause*) It was all right when Vassily was a child. Even more than all right, remember?

Sven Very clearly.

Gregor I suppose I felt I could have let him love me then without any danger.

Sven What danger?

Gregor Danger to me, my way of life, to my universe. But to be loved and worshipped by a grown boy — and by this boy above all ... Oh, no. I will take any risk, you know that Sven, but not the risk of being so close to the pure in heart "... And virtue entered into him." Isn't that from the Bible? Then there's your answer. If I wanted to make my son hate me instead of loving me it's because I can, at least, cope with hatred. I don't feel it for anyone or anything but I can understand and even relish it. But love is a commodity I can't afford. Was that a bad thing to say?

Sven Most fathers would think so.

Gregor Do you like your two boys?

Sven Oh, yes.

Gregor And they love you?

Sven From time to time.

Gregor I wonder if I am a very bad man.

Sven Oh, no. To be bad you must at least have some idea of what badness is.

Gregor (*with interest*) And I don't? Perhaps not. And yet I have a conscience. I must have, or I wouldn't have tried so hard to drive it away.

Sven (*smiling*) When did you have a conscience?

Gregor It came in human shape. And I did drive it away — five years ago. Sven? Am I what Vassily called me? Am I — nothing?

Sven You're Gregor Antonescu.

Florence comes down the steps and knocks on the front door

And being so, I think you had better get out of the line of sight of this door before I open it.

Gregor In God's name, why? An hour ago, yes. But not now. (*He faces the door*) Go on, Sven — open the door!

Sven opens the door to reveal Florence. In her three years as Countess Antonescu her accent has acquired some cosmopolitan flourishes, but is still basically English plebeian

Oh! It's you.

Florence comes into the living-room

Florence Well, what's all this about?

Gregor (*kissing her*) How are you, my love?

Florence Worried to death, since you ask. Do you know what I just heard from John? That you'd been arrested by the FBI and carted off to jail. Imagine my feelings.

Gregor I'm happy to show you, in person, that it isn't true.

Florence Yes, but imagine my feelings hearing a thing like that. And then there was another one John heard — that you disguised yourself as a steward and gone off on the Aquitania ——

Gregor (*to Sven*) Who is John?

Sven The Countess' chauffeur.

Gregor Personal or from the pool?

Florence (*slighted*) Personal. You said I could have a personal — and I told you the one I was getting.

Gregor So you did. Well, my dear, if he alarms you with these sorts of rumours, you'll have to fire him.

Florence I can't very well fire him ——

Gregor Ah, yes. You told me that too.

Florence I wish you'd tell me now what's going on.

Gregor I gather you didn't come by subway.

Florence No. I wouldn't. I told Sergei if he was going to get me into a subway he's going to have to knock me unconscious first ——

Gregor And he didn't?

Florence (*ignoring him, talking to Sven*) Well, I mean, it was so silly. Disguising me as someone ordinary and going down secret staircases — it was all *tout ce qu'il y a de plus* Warner Brothers. *N'est-ce pas*, Sven?

Sven You are here, Countess. That is all that matters.

Florence *Merci, mon cher.* Well, what kind of place is this when it's at home?

Gregor It's a basement apartment in Greenwich Village. Rather a smart thing to have these days. Sven, would you give the Countess that cheque for her to sign.

Sven gets a chequebook from his briefcase

Florence *Another* cheque?

Sven hands her the cheque and a pen

Blank, as usual. I've signed about twenty of these in the last three weeks. Just how much *are* you snitching from the foundation?

Sven and Gregor laugh

Why are you laughing?

Gregor The word "snitch" has a certain amusing association.

Florence Well, I hope there's enough left for my Maternity Centre.

Gregor Never fear, my dear. A cause so near your heart must not suffer. You may have to wait a few weeks to settle some bills, no more — Sven, would you add your signature?

Florence (*with alarm*) But the sub-committee has promised the contractors a cheque by the weekend.

Gregor Sail to Paris, then, my dear, before the weekend and don't answer any calls. Sven, would you send those cables?

Sven In cipher?

Gregor Yes.

Florence Listen, you're not involving me in anything fishy, are you?

Gregor Fishy? The Antonescu Foundation? The greatest charitable organization in the world? And you, the world's greatest philanthropist? Fishy. How could you think such a thing, my dear. (*To Sven*) Give me the file on the Mussolini loan.

Sven hands him a file from his briefcase and then goes into the bedroom, where throughout the ensuing scene, he will be busy with pen, paper and a code book

Gregor politely kisses Florence as he passes her, goes to a chair and begins to study the file. He never subsequently takes his eyes from it except at the moment indicated. But his replies to Florence are perfectly alert. One should feel that of his immense faculty of concentration he has relegated to Florence's conversation roughly one percent, and that percentage is proving perfectly sufficient

Florence (*looking round*) Well, which one does this apartment belong to?

Gregor Which one?

Florence (*impatiently*) Which girl friend?

Gregor No girl friend, my dear. If anything you might call it a boy friend ——

Florence Don't give me that. They say a lot of things about you — and most of them are true — but that's one thing they *can't* say. Come on. Come clean, for once.

Gregor I always come clean with you, my love.

Florence Like hell you do. (*Growing angry*) I'm your lawfully wedded wife, aren't I?

Gregor Indeed you are.

Florence OK. Then tell me who this place belongs to.

Gregor A young man I happen to know very well. You don't at all and very likely never will. There is no reason whatever for you to concern yourself about him or for me to give you his name.

Florence Yes. That's the sort of answer I've got used to these last three years. Well, here's another question for you — and this time I'd like a proper answer, please.

Gregor If I can give it to you, I will.

Florence You wouldn't like to look at me while I ask it, I suppose?

Gregor Of course, my dear. (*He puts his fingernail on the exact spot in the file he has reached and looks at her*) I should have asked you anyway to forgive my bad manners in studying these figures while talking to you, but time is rather important to me tonight.

Florence Oh, yes. We all know about the famous powers of concentration. Read a balance sheet, dictate to a secretary, speak on the telephone and make love to your wife — all at the same time ——

Gregor (*after a pause, very quietly*) What is your question, my love?

Florence It's the same one I ask most Mondays. Who spent the weekend with you on Long Island?

Gregor Sven, his wife, two children, William and Sergei, of course — and then a lot of people were coming and going from New York. There's been rather a big crisis on, you see.

Florence Crisis? I'll say there's a crisis. Do you think I enjoyed having photographers on the penthouse terrace this morning — peeping through my bedroom windows?

Gregor I'm sure any photographs they took of you were delightful, and equally sure they were only of you.

Florence Fat lot you'd care if they weren't.

Gregor I'd care a great deal.

Florence Only because of the publicity.

Gregor (*looking up voluntarily*) I'd care a great deal. (*He stares at her quietly and gravely for a moment, and then looks down at his file again*)

Florence Here we go again — switching everything round on to me. Well — there was no-one in my bedroom this morning — get that — and there hasn't been the whole month we've been in New York.

Gregor Except, I presume, John.

Florence (*furiously*) He doesn't stay all night.

Gregor I'm delighted to hear it.

Florence I'm not having my maids catch me with him. I've a good deal more *savoir faire* than that.

Gregor I'm quite sure you have, my dear.

Florence I'm getting side-tracked again. I know why they call you a genius. It's a genius for side-tracking people — nothing else — which of the girls went down for the weekend?

Gregor No girl, my dear.

Florence I expect it was the one who went last weekend. That Follies girl. She seems the current head of the New York harem.

Gregor (*looking up*) If there was a New York harem — if there were a London, Paris or Bucharest harem — if there were indeed any harem at all — it would always be you who would be at the head of it, my dear.

Florence Yes. Thank you very much. That just about sums up my position. Head of the Antonescu harem. And why am I the head? Because I'm the only one with the ring and the title. I'm only the something head. What's the word?

Gregor Titular.

Florence Titular head, that's all I am. All I'm really good for is sex and signatures, isn't that right?

Gregor Oh, no. Your conversation is often very stimulating indeed, my dear.

Florence But I'm not the head because you like me best of the bunch, I know that.

Gregor But I do like you best of the bunch, dear heart.

Florence Well, why a wife? Do you ever treat me like a wife?

Gregor's head is bent again over his file

A real wife, not just poor old Flo, the ex-typist, the London lay — carted round the world, dressed up to kill and calling herself Countess, because three years ago you decided to have yourself a good laugh by waving your magic wand and making all her silly dreams come true — plus giving her the name so you could use it for your Foundation — (*Pause*) Gregor! Look at me again.

Gregor puts his finger precisely on the file and looks up politely

I'm the wife of the greatest financier in the world, yes?

Gregor Since there is no other financier present to hear me — yes.

Florence Well, imagine my feelings these last few days ——

Gregor You have already asked me to do that tonight, my dear, twice ——

Florence Don't give me the sarcasm. This is serious. How do you think I've been feeling stuck up in that dreary apartment reading those great blazing headlines and not even able to talk to you?

Patiently, Gregor puts down his file, having marked a place in pencil, gets up and goes over to her. He puts his hands in an affectionate gesture on her shoulders and kisses her forehead

Gregor I am happy to tell you that the crisis is over.
Florence No kidding?
Gregor No kidding.
Florence Well, I'm not surprised. I knew you'd come through it. Well, everyone I spoke to who knows you said you would. (*Plaintively*) But you do see I had the right to be worried ——
Gregor Every right in the world.
Florence (*seriously*) No. Just a wife's right. I wasn't being jealous just now when I asked you which one came down for the weekend. Well, not jealous in the usual way. I just felt that if you were in trouble it ought to be *my* shoulder you cried on, and not one of the others.
Gregor As it happens, I cried on none.
Florence I didn't mean that literally, dear. To see *you* crying, that'll be the day. I meant you might be wanting a bit of comfort ——
Gregor (*fondling her*) I asked you to come here tonight, didn't I?
Florence (*not angrily*) Don't give me that. I know why you asked me tonight. Just that signature. Sergei gave it away.
Gregor Naughty Sergei.
Florence Gregor — I *could* love you, if you gave me the chance.
Gregor I shall give you the chance, my dear, if you care to wait. (*He looks at his watch*) In about an hour's time. Forgive me now. (*He walks away from her back to his chair where he resumes reading*)
Florence (*plaintively*) I didn't mean that kind of love ...

*Basil comes down the steps and flings the front-door open. His face is a mask. He is holding two papers—*New York Daily Mirror *and* New York Daily News, *early editions. He moves in to the living-room and stands facing his father, his back to us, and unfolds the papers so that Gregor can read the headlines*

Gregor's own face now becomes a mask. Basil puts the papers down on the sofa and turns abruptly to pour himself a drink

Florence (*seeing the headlines*) No. Oh, no ——

She makes a move to pick up the papers, but Gregor's icy voice stops her

Gregor (*icily*) Would you ask Sven to come in, please.

Florence moves to the bedroom door

Florence Sven — come in quick — something awful — he wants you —

Sven runs into the living-room

Gregor (*quietly, to Sven*) Vassily has just brought in two papers. I imagine they are early editions of the tabloids. One headline seems to read "Antonescu – Indictment Sought". The other says "Antonescu. Arrest Imminent." Would you read the headline stories please and tell me what they mean?

Sven snatches up the papers

Sven (*savagely to Basil*) Is this your doing?
Basil How could it be? I haven't been out of a bar except to buy those.
Gregor (*gently*) But of course it isn't Vassily.

Sven continues to read. Gregor watches him without apparent emotion, but he is gripping the arms of his chair and the mask of impassivity is beginning to crack

Sven (*at length*) The Bank of the City of London has applied to Scotland Yard for a warrant for your arrest.
Gregor The Bank of the City of London?
Sven If they succeed there will have to be extradition proceedings over here ——
Gregor The Bank of the City of London?
Sven (*reading*) "The Bank issued no details but it is understood the charges will relate to certain securities deposited by Antonescu as collateral for a loan in 1929."

Sven looks at Gregor enquiringly. Gregor stares back at him blankly

What securities are those, G.A.?

There is no reply. Gregor continues to stare at Sven blankly

(*Urgently*) G.A., — what securities did you deposit at the Bank in 1929?

Another pause

G.A.? ——
Gregor (*smiling*) Nothing.

Sven (*loudly*) G.A.,–you did raise a loan from that Bank in 1929. I remember
it. It was over six million pounds. (*Pause*) So you must have pledged some
collateral. What was it?
Gregor Nothing.

Sven turns hopelessly away, throwing the papers down

Wait. Wait. (*In a perfectly normal voice*) So sorry, Sven — dear fellow.
Forgive me. I was talking nonsense. It's so hard sometimes to remember
and when one can't think ... And after what Vassily said earlier ...
(*Suddenly*) Six million one hundred and twenty-six thousand ——
Sven That was the *amount* of the loan G.A. What did you *pledge* for it?
Gregor (*after a pause*) Some bonds. I'll remember in a moment, dear boy.
(*Plaintively*) Don't plague me ——
Sven G.A.,— we must get through to London tonight. But before we do there
is one thing I must know. These securities you pledged five years ago —
were they forged?

There is a pause during which Gregor remains utterly still

Gregor (*with difficulty*) If I could move I wouldn't sit still in this chair to
receive insults. But you see ... I can't move.

Sven moves briskly to Gregor and tries to raise him from it

Sven (*briskly*) Vassily — help me ——

Basil joins him

Take his other arm. It's easier if we get him on his feet.
Basil Has this happened before?
Sven Yes.
Basil Should I get a doctor?
Sven No.

*They succeed in getting Gregor on his feet. He is conscious but apparently
oblivious of his surroundings. Supported by Basil and Sven he walks with
difficulty, but without resisting his helpers, towards the bedroom*

Florence I didn't know this happened. I've never seen him like this.
(*Hysterically*) We must get a doctor — now. (*During the following, she
sits in the living-room, frightened*)
Sven No, Countess. Not yet. We may have to take the risk later, but not yet.

Florence You mean — because of the police?

Sven (*to Florence*) He can recover from these things very quickly. No need yet to take an unnecessary risk.

As Gregor reaches the bed he suddenly pushes Sven and Basil away

Lie down on the bed, G.A.

Gregor The telephone is ringing. It will be Rome. I want to speak to them, please.

Basil Later, father. Lie down now.

Gregor (*at length, gently*) Vassily, dear boy — I know something has happened to me, but I have to speak to Rome. I have all the figures in my mind. Six percent — six and a half percent. (*He holds his head and then turns pleadingly to Basil*) Vassily — six or six and a half?

Basil (*gently but firmly*) Father — you are ill. Please rest ——

Gregor But if Rome is on the line ——

Basil There's no-one on the line, father.

Gregor No-one? I thought the telephone —— (*He points*)

Basil No. It didn't ring.

Gregor Are you quite sure?

Basil Father, I'm quite sure the telephone didn't ring.

Gregor nods slowly, then assisted by Sven and Basil, lies on the bed

Gregor Six and a *half* percent, Sven — I'm all right. The figures are still quite clear.

Sven Yes, G.A. Just lie there for a moment. Can you sleep?

Gregor I expect so. What's Vassily doing here?

Sven This is his apartment, G.A. You're lying on his bed.

Gregor Oh, yes, of course. How foolish. It's very good of you, Vassily, to let me rest on your bed.

Basil I'm going to turn out the light, father. You must try and sleep. (*He turns the lights out in the bedroom*)

Gregor (*murmuring in the dark*) Thank you, my boy.

Sven, after a look at Gregor, goes back into the living-room where Florence is still sitting

Florence How is he?

Sven shrugs, picks up the newspapers and sits to read them

I'm sorry I wasn't more help, but I can't bear illness. You do understand that, don't you?

Sven (*without looking up*) Yes, Countess, perfectly.

In the bedroom, Gregor is lying on his back, still and apparently asleep. Basil approaches the darkened bed, looking down at his father

Gregor (*suddenly speaking quite clearly*) What a sweet revenge for you — dearest boy.

Basil moves away from the bed, out of Gregor's sight and watches him from there. There are no further sign of life from Gregor. Basil goes quickly into the living-room, plainly in a state of deep distress

Basil (*to Sven*) A man came into the bar with those papers — I saw the headlines and went out and bought them.

Sven, still reading, nods

Because I thought at least he ought to be warned.
Sven Quite right.
Basil I wasn't to know, was I?
Sven No. Of course not.
Basil Five years ago he was healthy — much healthier than me.
Sven Dear boy, you weren't to know. And he would have learnt the news anyway.
Basil But not from me.

Sven, for the first time interested in what he is saying, looks up at him

All right! I was mad as hell at him — after what he did to me. When I went out I was going to get a room and never come back again — not ever. But I did come back because of those goddamn papers — nobody told me that I could give him a stroke.
Sven (*at length; puzzled and rather amused by this outburst*) He had an attack like this quite recently. I'm sure he'll be perfectly all right in a few hours ——
Basil He says it's revenge ——
Sven Of course he does.
Basil Do you?
Sven I really hadn't bothered to think about it. Now that you force me to, I'd say merely that if it wasn't revenge, it should have been.
Basil (*fiercely*) But, Sven, *was* it?
Sven What an extraordinary boy you are, Vassily. Why, I wonder, were you born to G.A. of all people.

Florence stirs

Oh, you haven't been introduced, have you ——

Basil I'm sorry. I knew who you were. I've seen photographs.

Florence Vassily? Not the — son, Vassily?

Basil Yes.

Florence Then you must be the son he said died five years ago.

Basil He said that?

Florence Not just to me. To everyone ——

Basil Well, I suppose — to him — I did die five years ago.

Florence You ran away?

Basil Yes. I did. Will you excuse me? (*He turns to Sven*) There's no point in reading those. They won't tell you anything. What he pledged to the Bank of the City of London for his six million pounds was exactly what he said — nothing.

Sven There must have been collateral.

Basil (*hopelessly*) Yes. A receipt from them for some bonds to the credit of Antonescu Holdings.

Sven International Bank of Liechtenstein? That's a new one on me.

Basil I'm surprised.

Sven He never told me everything.

Basil He told me. He made a point of telling me at my coming of age party.

Sven This Bank at Liechtenstein — it's the usual thing?

Basil Yes. Like all the four hundred other Antonescu Banks. A set of portable books, a board of directors who don't know what they're directing, and a local crooked accountant paid a hundred dollars a week — or has the salary gone up since my time?

Sven Trebled, quadrupled. Why didn't *you* make your fortune, while there was still time?

Basil The way you have?

Sven (*genially*) Perfectly permissible if said to me. But unwise if said to the police.

Basil says nothing. Florence looks in bewilderment from one to the other

Florence But what's he done? I don't understand.

Sven (*firmly*) Countess, I realize this is all very distressing for you. Why don't you go in next door and watch over your husband as a good wife should?

Florence goes reluctantly into the bedroom and hovers at the doorway

Basil How has he got away with it for so long?

Sven (*shrugging*) Confidence.

Basil (*hopelessly*) "Liquidity and confidence."

Sven Until yesterday, when the Bank of the City of London evidently felt it time to inspect the Antonescu account rather more closely.

Florence He's asleep. I can't bear illness. (*She drifts back into the room to a chair and sits*)

Sven Other banks, too, I'm afraid, will be doing the same thing. How many other transactions of this kind do you know of?

Basil Dozens. And since 1930 you must know of dozens more.

Sven Oh, no. I never knew of anything actually — *criminal.* (*He spreads his hands*) Obviously, dearest Vassily, I couldn't have, or I wouldn't have stayed with him, would I?

There is a pause while Basil stares at Sven

Basil Don't desert him, Sven. Don't *you* desert him.

Sven My dear Vassily. You must know that I have served your father with the deepest and truest devotion ——

Basil But miracles must have happened in the last five years to let him get away with what he has — can't you and I make another miracle happen for him now?

Sven looks at Basil with faint amusement but with greater sympathy

Sven (*at length*) Poor Vassily.

Basil Don't say that. That's not a criminal in there, that's a great man. Who gave roads to Yugoslavia?

Sven (*interrupting the familiar*) — and electricity to Hungary? Your father of course.

Florence is fiddling with the radio, trying to get a news broadcast

Basil (*realizing he is being laughed at*) Well, he did, and much more besides. What's so wrong in getting money to circulate freely from rich countries to poor countries?

Sven I'd measure it at about fifteen years hard labour.

Basil But it's the system that should be on trial, not father.

Sven Yes, yes. The system ——

Basil (*passionately*) Have you heard about his childhood in Bucharest?

Sven Oh, yes. Many times ——

In the bedroom, Gregor stirs from his lying position and sits on the bed, swaying his head slowly from side to side, as if trying to clear his brain. After a time, he stops, and stares at the floor, still sitting but motionless

Florence turns up the radio's volume

Florence Quiet. I've got some news.

On the radio: "…. one of the biggest financial scandals of all time, dwarfing even Kreuger, Loewenstein and Insull. The warrant held by the FBI for the arrest of Gregor Antonescu——"

Florence ⎱ (*together*) ⎰ Oh my God ——
Basil   Warrant?

On the radio: "—will be executed as soon as the missing financier, who is believe to now be still hiding somewhere on Manhattan Island, is located and captured. All ports, airfields and borders are being …"

Basil signs for Florence to switch off the radio. She does. Basil turns anxiously to Sven

Basil Mark Herries has given them this address.
Sven No. Oh no. Herries wouldn't want to be implicated. (*With a faint smile*) Beside he'd hardly give them *this* address.
Basil (*to Florence*) Did you come here by car?
Florence Yes, but they were only reporters — I mean they weren't policemen ——
Basil (*turning back to Sven*) That's how they know he's in New York.
Sven I imagine.
Basil We can't be sure at least one didn't follow her here. They said Manhattan Island. We'll have to get him out of here at once.
Sven Where?
Basil Out of the country. Mexico. He can stay the night at Carol Penn's. I've got a friend with a car I can borrow. It's an old coupe — so if we are to get him into Mexico it will be much more suitable than anything you can organize. I can drive him. Sven, how much cash has he on him?
Sven He never carries any. (*He pulls out a wallet and hands it to Basil*) There's over a thousand there ——
Basil What about you?
Sven Thank you. I'm provided for.

Basil goes into the bedroom, switching on the lights. Gregor looks at him from his sitting position

Florence Do I have to stay?

Sven He might need you.
Basil (*to Gregor*) Are you feeling better father?
Florence I don't know what for. There's nothing I can do to help around here.
Basil (*to Gregor*) Shouldn't you be lying down? Father, I'm sorry, but this
news has to be given to you suddenly. Can you hear and understand what
I'm saying? And are you strong enough to hear it?

Gregor nods slowly. It is plain that he does hear and understand

We've just heard on the radio that the FBI have a warrant out for your arrest.

Gregor nods again, slowly, but quite calmly, still evidently understanding

We think they may know of this place, and so I'm going out now to get a
car and move you to another apartment. It belongs to Carol, the girl you met
earlier tonight.
Gregor (*nods again; very softly*) Does she know that it's an offence in law
to harbour a wanted criminal?

*Pause. Gregor continues to look up at Basil quietly and gravely. Basil smiles
at his father, suddenly, and for the first time that evening.*

Basil I know, father, and if she doesn't I'll tell her.
Gregor (*quietly*) Would you ask Sven to come in?

Basil nods and goes into the living-room

Basil (*to Sven*) He wants you.

Sven goes to the bedroom

Florence How is he?

Basil goes to the front-door

Basil Better. We'll get him into the car, OK.
Florence Why did you ever leave him?
Basil He made me.

Basil exits

In the bedroom Gregor is looking at Sven with a faint, wry smile

Gregor What the boy said is true? There's a warrant out for me over here?

Sven nods

Yes, of course, Vassily doesn't lie.

Sven He's taking you to his girl tonight in a borrowed two-seater and tomorrow he's going to try and drive you down to the Mexican border.

Gregor (*with a faint laugh*) Mexican border? Vassily always did suffer from an over-romantic mind.

Sven Have you ever made plans to meet this emergency?

Gregor Yes. But they don't involve escape. (*Pause. He looks at the floor and shivers slightly*) Is it cold in here?

Sven It's a warm night ——

Gregor Put something over my shoulders, would you? — there's a good fellow.

Sven puts Basil's dinner-jacket round Gregor's shoulders

I've left you the controlling interest in Manson Radios. If I were you, I'd hold on. For a couple of days they'll be worthless, but things will pick up one day and there's a patent on a new television process that could be valuable.

Sven Won't you at least let Vassily try?

Gregor How long would it take him to drive me to the Mexican border?

Sven (*shrugging*) Five or six days.

Gregor Five or six days alone in a two-seater with my conscience? No. (*He shivers again*) Where is Sergei, at this moment?

Sven At his apartment.

Gregor Conveniently close.

Sven (*after a pause*) Convenient for what?

Gregor For you to go there and borrow a gun. (*Pause*) Will you do that for me, dear boy? (*Silence. A flash of old authority*) Do that for me, please, Sven.

Sven makes no move

I don't really need it, you know — there are other ways. But it would be a great favour to me to let me have this gun with me tonight.

Sven (*at length*) All right, G.A. (*He goes to into the living- room, picks up his hat and briefcase and goes to the front door*)

Florence, alarmed by his apparent desertion, is on her feet quickly

Florence You're not leaving?
Sven I have something to do.
Florence Do I have to stay?
Sven You're his wife.

Sven exits quickly

Florence subsides gloomily into a chair. Gregor, in the bedroom, is staring at the floor. Suddenly he lifts his head

Gregor Florence? Florence? (*He gets off the bed and staggers to the living-room door*)

Florence rises, startled

I thought you'd gone.
Florence Sven told me to stay.
Gregor I'm glad. I'm very glad. (*He holds out his arms*) Come here — (*They embrace*) My darling, I'm so happy you stayed. Earlier tonight didn't you say you wanted to be a wife — a real wife?
Florence Yes.
Gregor Even the wife of a hunted man?
Florence What have you done, Gregor?
Gregor It would be a little complicated to explain. I must sit down. Do you mind? (*He flops onto a chair*)

Florence stands, staring at him cautiously

You came here by car, didn't you? (*He grasps Florence's hand*)
Florence (*letting her hand be grasped but not responding*) Yes. The Lincoln.
Gregor Is it still there?
Florence I expect so.
Gregor Have a look.

Florence goes to the front-door

See if there are any people hanging around — or if there's a policeman ——
Florence (*startled*) Policemen? They won't be after *me*?
Gregor (*patiently*) No, my dear. Only after me.

Florence goes out, checks from the top of the basement steps and returns

Florence Yes. John's still there. And there's no-one about.

Gregor nods and attempts to get to his feet

Gregor Would you help? (*He flops back, exhausted*) It's no good. Later, you'll have to get him to come back here and help me in.
Florence You're not going to use my car for a getaway?
Gregor No, not for a getaway. At least only from this place ——
Florence What for, then?
Gregor To drive somewhere. Perhaps to Washington Square. We could sit on a bench for a few moments together and then, perhaps, you could be with me when —— (*he stops*)

Pause. Florence stares at him in horror

Florence When what? When what? When you kill yourself? Is that what you mean?
Gregor I'm not going to be arrested. I decided that years ago. Thank you for caring.
Florence (*in horror*) And you want me there? There, when you actually do it?

Pause

Gregor Perhaps that was not a good idea. (*With sudden anguish*) I just crave for some human being to be with me now, that's all.
Florence There's Vassily.
Gregor (*fiercely*) Not Vassily. I'll be gone before he comes back anyway.
Florence But he loves you, he's the one you want with you tonight, Gregor. Not me. I don't know why you should suddenly want it to be *me*.
Gregor (*harshly*) Because you're here — because you're my wife — because that dress you're wearing and those jewels and that Lincoln and the chauffeur are all mine — because even your title is mine — bought and paid for by me — and because I think you owe me at least one hour of my last night on earth.
Florence But it *should* be Vassily.
Gregor No! Poor Vassily. Whatever happens I won't ask him to hold my hand and lend me a shoulder to cry on. (*After a pause*) *You* said that, didn't you, earlier? Something about a shoulder to cry on. Didn't you say it should be yours?
Florence Yes, I suppose I did.
Gregor Well?
Florence (*plaintively*) I don't want to get involved, Gregor.

Pause

Gregor (*at length*) I see.

Florence Don't blame me.

Gregor I don't.

Florence Perhaps it could have been different, if you'd wanted it before. But you never did, did you? Not till now, and now — well — it's just too late, that's all.

Pause

Gregor Antonescu-training, I see. (*Pause, then briskly*) Well, goodbye then, my dear.

Florence You do understand?

Gregor Very clearly. I've left you a cash sum of one million dollars. (*Bitterly*) Whatever happens, that at least, can't be involved. Sven knows where it is.

Florence Sven? Was it wise to trust Sven? Personally I wouldn't trust him further than I could see him.

Gregor looks at her with a faint smile

It's not just the money. You know that. It's just that I wouldn't like to see him get away with anything.

Gregor I understand perfectly, my dear.

Florence (*standing above him, looking down on him*) Goodbye, then.

Gregor (*without looking at her*) Goodbye, my dear.

Florence moves to offer a farewell kiss

Don't kiss me, please.

Florence moves to the front-door

Florence I'm sorry, Gregor. Really, I'm sorry. You see —— (*She can find no words for her explanation*)

Gregor, sitting stiff and still, merely looks at her

Florence exits

Gregor, left alone, begins to shiver. Then he rises and crosses with difficulty to the drinks trolley. He pours himself out a drink and drinks it

Basil enters

Basil Well done.

Gregor Dear boy.

Basil Ready to go?

Gregor No, I'm not going. At least not with you, dearest Vassily.

Basil But I've got the car.

Gregor I'm most deeply touched at all you've tried to do for me. Believe it. But Sven has organized something perhaps a little more — secure. A private aeroplane.

Basil (*deeply disappointed*) Tonight?

Gregor Oh, of course tonight. Now, in fact. I was just waiting for you — to say goodbye and thank you — before getting on my way.

Basil Are you fit enough to travel tonight?

Gregor No.

Basil Can't I help at all?

Gregor No.

Basil I really want to, you know.

Gregor Yes. I do know. Why do you drink? Is it because of me?

Basil No. I think it's because of me. No strength of will. Do you remember, father? The weak go to the wall.

Gregor And the strong fly to Mexico.

Basil I didn't mean that.

Gregor I know you didn't. (*Pause*) How much harm have I done you, Vassily?

Basil (*murmuring*) Not much.

Gregor Be truthful with me, please. Have I ruined your life?

Basil No. I am what you've always said I am — soft, that's all. I'll get by. When you get to Mexico, where will you go?

Gregor Sven has made plans.

Basil Wherever you end up, will you remember that I'm always here to help you?

Gregor Yes, I will.

Basil This is one — contact — the police won't trace. Basil Anthony — piano player and songwriter ——

Gregor Do you write good songs?

Basil I think so. The publishers don't.

Gregor I think you will write good songs.

Basil Thank you, father.

Gregor Don't you want a drink?

Basil No.

Gregor Interesting.

Basil Why?

Gregor Our roles are becoming reversed. Who is now the strong and who the weak?

Basil I could never be strong.

Gregor I don't know. But something tells me you won't find it too hard, in the future, to give up the bottle. Tell me, how much joy will there be in the Socialist ranks at my downfall?

Basil Quite a lot, I suppose. But if you fail, it will be because the system has failed, not you. And if you rose to be the greatest capitalist of all time, it was because, instinctively, you had to get your revenge on society ——

Gregor (*mildly*) Why? Whatever had society done to me?

Basil Starved you in Bucharest. Sent you out as a child to beg in the streets ——

Gregor Did I tell you that?

Basil I don't remember. It's in every book about you ——

Gregor Is it? Obviously no-one has bothered to check up. Now, I imagine, they will. How amusing.

Pause. Basil, in sudden panic, goes to pour himself a drink, his back to Gregor

Yes, have that. But let it be your last, dearest Vassily. I have no further illusions to break for you. I never had to beg for anything in my life.

Basil (*without turning*) That must be a lie.

Gregor Why, at this moment, should I tell you a lie?

Basil Because you always have told me lies ——

Gregor Oh, no, it's the truth I have always told you. It's you who have always interpreted them as lies. My father says he's a swindler. Then it's the system that made him so. My father has defrauded hundreds of thousands of people out of their hard earned savings, but he's still a great man — the saviour of post-war Europe. (*Very gently*) Did it never occur to you that I might enjoy that title — just for itself alone? That my reward isn't in the fact of having brought roads to Yugoslavia and electricity to Hungary — it's in the ... It's in the fact of it being known.

Basil (*indistinctly*) God damn you! God damn you!

Gregor Poor Vassily! Always so easy to make you cry.

Sven comes down the steps, opens the front-door abruptly and stands watching the two

Gregor looks at him enquiringly, Sven nods. Gregor motions with his head to the bedroom. Sven goes in, carrying his briefcase and closes the door quietly. Gregor stares at his son in silence for a moment

Well, dearest boy, you must go now. Sven and I have to make plans and we have very little time.

Basil But can't I stay and help?

Gregor Better not.

Basil I had hoped … (*He stops uncertainly*) I had hoped you might allow me to come with you.

Gregor Dear God, what a boy! Isn't there anything I can do to kill it?

Basil No. Not anything. But why do you have to try?

Gregor I don't know. (*Shrugging*) Perhaps because — having had to live all my life without a conscience — it would be rather — unmanly — to acquire one now. You must go and return that two-seater to your friend.

Pause

Basil (*desperately*) Isn't there *any* way … Isn't there any way at all, father — I can be of use to you at this moment?

Gregor No. (*Gravely looking at him*) I wish there were. (*He holds out his arms*)

Basil walks slowly to him and Gregor embraces him. The contrast with the other paternal embrace we have seen is very marked, it is the face of a deeply anguished man staring at us, sightlessly from over Basil's shoulder. Then Gregor, with a brisk change of tone, pats him on the back

Marry that girl. And give up that tiresome habit of drinking.

Basil nods. Pause

Basil You'll come through, father, you always do.

Gregor Thank you, dear boy. And never, in future, let the truth make you cry.

Basil exits

Gregor closes the door after him. Then he walks to the bedroom

(*To Sven*) You've brought it?

Sven Yes.

Gregor Let me have it, please. Come on Sven, give me the gun.

Sven One moment, G.A.

Gregor sits, shivering at moments. Sven goes quickly into the living-room and goes to the desk drawer and pulls out a piece of paper and a pen. Inside the drawer, his attention is caught by a small snapshot. He examines it and slips it into his pocket. He returns to the bedroom and methodically picks up a telephone book, pushes Gregor's knees together, lays a sheet of paper on the telephone book and hands it to Gregor

Can you write with that on your knee?

Gregor (*staring at him; then laughs*) Ah, Antonescu-training, too. (*He unscrews his pen; wearily*) Who to?

Sven (*firmly*) To me.

Gregor Correctly it should be to Florence.

Sven I'm your best friend.

Gregor (*quietly; after a pause*) And you have the gun. (*He begins to write*) "Dear Sven" — can I avoid the cliché of "this is the only way out"? (*After a moment's thought*) Why not? It's true. (*He writes*) Would you be kind enough to get that overcoat of mine from the other room and put it round my shoulders? I don't know why, but I still feel cold.

Sven does so. Gregor continues to write

I have written: "Dear Sven, this is the only way out. I took this revolver earlier tonight from Sergei's apartment when neither of you were looking, with the intention of shooting myself. I am sorry to leave affairs in such a mess. Goodbye, my dearest friend."

Sven You've signed it?

Gregor Yes, "Gregor".

Sven Then would you please add this P.S.

Gregor obediently takes up his pen

"You will be appalled to hear of the many criminal transactions ——"

Gregor laughs harshly and sharply, but continues to write

" — which, during my life, I have perpetrated ——"

Gregor May I say "done"?

Sven Of course.

Gregor (*writing*) Thank you. After all, it *will* be published ——

Sven "In every single one of these transactions —"

Gregor (*writing*) "In every single one of — *them* —" Better.

Sven "You have been the innocent dupe."

Gregor (*writing*) "You, my dearest, dearest Sven —" a little touch of sentiment never hurts, "have been the innocent dupe." (*He hands the paper to Sven*)

Sven You might just put your signature to it, would you?

Gregor (*doing so*) It's not usual with a P.S. (*He hands the paper again*) Don't you think it might look a little — forced?

Sven Better than looking forged. (*He puts the note in his pocket*)

Gregor Absolutely correct.

Sven pulls a revolver wrapped in a hankie from his briefcase and hands it silently to Gregor

Is it loaded?
Sven Yes. (*Pointing*) You cock it here.
Gregor I see. The mouth is best, isn't it?
Sven So they say.
Gregor Kreuger shot himself through the heart. But I think he was lucky. There are some chances not even I will take. (*After a pause*) On the other hand I don't like to be beaten by Kreuger. (*He shivers again*)

Sven moves towards the door

You're not leaving?
Sven Surely it's better ——
Gregor I had hoped — I had hoped you might stay with me.
Sven Oh, no. Oh, no, G.A. You must see, I can't be involved. And with this letter ——
Gregor (*with difficulty*) Yes. Yes, of course. Goodbye, then.

Sven makes a move towards him

Don't touch me, do you mind? (*Smiling at him*) It nearly worked, didn't it? Another twenty-four hours and we'd have done it again.

Sven nods. As a sudden thought he takes out of his pocket the snapshot he found in the desk and hands it to Gregor

Sven I found this on the desk.
Gregor What is it?
Sven It's a snapshot of you and Vassily on a beach somewhere. He must have been about eight or nine, I think.
Gregor (*peering at it*) Yes, I remember. It was at Biarritz. There's something written on it. What is it?
Sven "To Vassily, from his father, with love". I thought you wouldn't want it found by the police.
Gregor The police won't find anything here.
Sven I see. I didn't know — where ——
Gregor How careless of him though! How typical! He calls himself Basil Anthony, American citizen, denies his father and keeps a photograph of him ——
Sven What shall I do with it?
Gregor Put it back, I suppose. It seem to have some value to him ——

Sven goes back into the living-room, puts the snapshot back in the drawer. Turns uncertainly back to the bedroom door

Go away, dearest fellow, if you're going.

Sven picks up his hat, gloves and briefcase and exits

Gregor gets up and moves into the living-room, turning out the bedroom light as he goes. In the living-room, he struggles into his overcoat, puts the revolver on the drinks trolley, sees his unfinished drink, and downs it. He puts on his hat and goes to the front door, as if to exit. He stops, and returns to the drinks trolley. He picks up the gun, goes back to the door, and switches off the lights. He opens the door and turns back to look at the room for the last time

Black-out

CURTAIN

FURNITURE AND PROPERTY LIST

ACT I

On stage: *In the living-room*
Chairs
Desk containing paper, screw-top pen, small snapshot
Drinks Trolley with bourbon, water and glasses
Waste-paper basket
Radio
Lamps
Pictures

In the kitchenette:
Kettle
Stove
Matches
Ice
Tray with cups
Coffee, cream and sugar

In the bedroom:
Bed with sheet and coverlet
Bedside table. *On it*: watch, telephone, telephone book, ashtray and
    cigarette for **Carol,** lipstick
On a hook: man's bathrobe
In a closet: trouser, brightly-coloured silk shirt for **Basil**

In the shower/lavatory:
Cup
Eyewash
Towel
Bath towel
Comb

Off stage: Newspaper
Briefcase containing chequebook and pen, file, paper, code book,
    revolver wrapped in a hankie for **Sven**
Biefcase containing statement, documents for **Beeston**
Bottle of Bourbon for **Basil**

Personal: **Basil:** key
                 Sven: watch, wallet containing a ten dollar bill, notebook and pen,
                 Herries: notebook and pen, card
                 Gregor: watch, pencil

ACT II

On stage: as ACT I

Off stage: *New York Daily Mirror* and *New York Daily News* for **Basil**

Personal: **Sven:** bottle of pills

LIGHTING PLOT

Practical fittings required: lamp
Composite setting comprising, living-room, kitchenette, bedroom, shower/lavatory.
1 exterior backing

ACT I

To open: General interior lighting throughout. Summer's evening light on exterior

Cue 1:	**Sven** puts on the lamp	(Page 21)
	Bring up practical lamp with covering spot	

ACT II

To open: General interior lighting throughout. Late evening light on exterior

Cue 2	**Basil** switches the lights out in the bedroom	(Page 51)
	Darken lights on bedroom	
Cue 3	**Basil** switches the lights on in the bedroom	(Page 55)
	Brighten lights on bedroom	
Cue 4	**Gregor** turns out the bedroom light	(Page 66)
	Darken lights on bedroom	
Cue 5	**Gregor** turns out the living-room lights	(Page 66)
	Darken lights on living-room/kitchenette	
Cue 6	**Gregor** turns to look at the room for one last time	(Page 66)
	Black-out	

EFFECTS PLOT

ACT I

Cue 1   **Carol** sings in the shower   (Page 2)
          Telephone rings

Cue 2   **Basil** puts on the radio   (Page 4)
          Strains of Guy Lombardo plays. Continue as dialogue pp 4-6

Cue 3   **Sven** switches off the radio   (Page 6)
          Cut radio

Cue 4   **Carol** switches on the radio   (Page 15)
          Music blares

Cue 5   **Carol** switches off the radio   (Page 15)
          Cut music

Cue 6   **Gregor:** " ...hearing it distorted."   (Page 15)
          Telephone rings

ACT II

Cue 7   **Florence** fiddles with the radio   (Page 54)
          Tuning and various radio station effects,
          *   eventually ending on a broadcast station*

Cue 8   **Florence** turns up the radio's volume   (Page 55)
          Increase radio's volume continue as dialogue p55

Cue 9   **Florence** turns off the radio   (Page 55)
          Cut radio